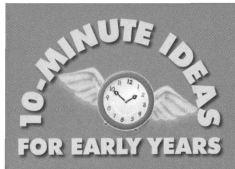

10-MINUTE IDEAS
FOR EARLY YEARS

Moving
and dancing

Beverley Michael

■ **Quick activities for any time of the day**

■ **Links to Early Learning Goals** ■ **Time-saving photocopiables**

Credits

Author
Beverley Michael

Editor
Susan Howard

Assistant Editor
Charlotte Ronalds

Series Designer
Anna Oliwa

Designer
Andrea Lewis

Cover Illustration
Craig Cameron/Art Collection

Illustrations
Cathy Hughes

Text © 2004
© 2004 Scholastic Ltd

Designed using Adobe InDesign

Published by Scholastic Ltd
Villiers House
Clarendon Avenue
Leamington Spa
Warwickshire
CV32 5PR

www.scholastic.co.uk

Printed by Bell & Bain

1 2 3 4 5 6 7 8 9   4 5 6 7 8 9 0 1 2 3

British Library Cataloguing-in-Publication Data
A catalogue record for this book is available from the British Library.

ISBN 0-439-97152-7

Contents

Introduction 5

Ourselves

Space stations 7
Choose a partner 8
Muscle power 9
Who's under the blanket? 10
Body bumps 11
Around and around 12
Beanbag ballet 13
Hands up 14
On the line 15
Hello, goodbye 16

The living world

Under the sea 17
Silly seasons 18
Mole in a hole 19
Autumn leaves 20
Butterflies and caterpillars 21
Swirling snow 22
Stormy seas 23
Let's fly 24
Dancing daisies 25
Tall trees 26

Let's pretend

Washday 27
Come to the circus 28
Fireworks 29
Flamenco 30
Cowboy capers 31
Monster mash 32
Blow, blow, pop! 33
Noah's Ark 34
Rain dance 35
All aboard 36

Playing games

Traffic lights 37
Pick and pass 38
Busy bees 39
Grumpy old bear 40
Sheep pen 41
Lily pads 42
Jet pilot 43
Magog the dragon 44
Over the mountain 45
Clothes dash 46

Contents

Action rhymes and songs

Body parts 47

Moon walk 48

The marmalade cat 49

Happy families 50

Ten fine soldiers 51

Alphabet actions........................ 52

The world keeps spinning.......... 53

Mean machines 54

Dancing feet 55

Jack-in-the-box 56

Traditional stories and rhymes

Incy Wincy Spider........................ 57

Cinderella's duster 58

Snow White 59

Gingerbread men 60

Twinkle, twinkle, little star 61

Three blind mice.......................... 62

Billy goats gruff 63

Nursery rhyme rhythms.............. 64

Little Red Riding Hood 65

Three little pigs 66

Photocopiables

Floppy Fiona 67

What are these hands doing? 68

Can you fly?................................. 69

The trees are growing tall............ 70

Under the big top 71

Monster moods 72

Noah and the big rain 73

Buzzing bees 74

Lily pad game 75

I have one head 76

Here comes daddy 77

I can..... 78

Twinkling stars 79

Sing the rhyme 80

Introduction

The activities in this book provide children with the opportunity to develop self-expression and creativity through dance, and to develop physical skills such as co-ordination, manipulation, body awareness and confidence, through movement. Children need time and space to develop these physical skills. Allow children sufficient opportunity to initiate their own moving and dancing games, both indoors and outdoors, through unstructured activities. Encouraging the children to take part in activities planned by the adult, such as those contained within this book, give a specific opportunity for teaching and learning.

Using the activities

The activities require little or no preparation and resources are kept to a minimum, thus making them excellent for immediate use. Emphasising the fun aspects of the activities will develop confidence and encourage participation by the children. Group sizes are recommended, but should be based upon the age and ability of the children and how much adult supervision is available.

Planning for the Stepping Stones and Early Learning Goals

Children need daily opportunities to use and develop their larger muscles by running, jumping, balancing, dancing and so on, and moving and dancing should be included in any planning of the curriculum. The ideas found in these pages can be used as individual activities or incorporated into wider planned themes and topics.

Stepping Stones and Early Learning Goals are included for each activity and all six Areas of Learning are covered. These Areas of Learning are shown in an abbreviated form in brackets at the bottom of each activity's 'Learning objectives' box: Personal, social and emotional development is PSED; Communication, language and literacy is CLL; Mathematical development is MD; Knowledge and understanding of the world is KUW; Physical develoment is PD, and Creative development is CD. However, these guidelines are not exclusive and every opportunity should be taken to introduce moving and dancing into other areas in order to expand the learning potential.

Assessment opportunities

When children take part in moving and dancing activities it gives the practitioner the opportunity to assess the following:
■ the child's development of the social skills of co-operation, turn taking, awareness of others, and the amount of involvement shown by each child when engaged in group games or activities which require a partner
■ the ability of the child to accept and abide by the rules of a game
■ the ability of the child to express their feelings and emotions creatively through dance and movement
■ the development of the child's physical skills, such as running, skipping, balancing, throwing and catching, and assessing what skills the child has already acquired and how to build on them
■ the child's spatial relationship with their environment and their knowledge and use of spatial language and response to the language of movement

■ the child's ability to respond to stimuli, such as story, rhyme and music through moving and dancing.

Setting up the environment

Advance planning and careful thought in preparing a suitable environment is essential before all moving and dancing activities.

■ Children need a clear area in which to explore their physical capabilities, for example, a large mat, a safe area outdoors or a room indoors where the furniture has been moved out of the way. If space is limited, make use of a local park, village hall or leisure centre.

■ You will need a collection of tapes or CDs for dancing to, including folk, rap, reggae, classical, orchestral, pop, jazz, choral, rock and nursery rhymes.

■ Collect a selection of musical percussion instruments, commercial or home-made, suitable for the children to dance to or use to beat out a rhythm.

■ Provide balls, hoops, skipping ropes and beanbags, and chalk for marking when outdoors, and keep a collection of floaty scarves, streamers, capes, wands, headbands and so on to use during dance sessions.

Multicultural links

Introduce children to music and dance from a variety of cultures. The Chinese New Year and Indian Divali, for example, can be used to inspire dance activities. Children of all ages will enjoy watching dancers and musicians of various ethnic origins perform for them. Traditional stories and songs from all over the world can be adapted for moving and dancing activities.

Safety

Always ensure that moving and dancing activities with groups of children travelling quickly are carefully supervised. Include as many available helpers as possible in the activities, particularly if younger children are involved.

Carry out a safety check of the environment. Make sure that any equipment used is in good working order and that the area is clear and free of potential dangers. Ensure that children are wearing appropriate clothing for the activity and have a supply available if necessary.

Home links

Ways to encourage parents and carers to become involved in their child's learning are suggested for each activity. As well as showing children that their home and childcare settings are linked, it demonstrates to parents and carers the value of moving and dancing activities in their child's development and how they can share them with their child.

How to use this book

The 10-minute activities can be used at a specific time as a regular part of the daily curriculum, whenever a short period of time becomes available during the day that needs to be filled productively, or if children become restless when inclement weather prevents outdoor play. The activities can be carried out as often as required as children enjoy the repetitiveness of moving and dancing games and the repetition will reinforce the skills introduced.

Photocopiable activity sheets are available for use alongside certain activities, together with suggestions for use, to further enhance learning.

Ourselves

Simple moving and dancing games are ideal for focusing the children on themselves. The activities in this chapter introduce the names of parts of the body and also help develop the children's ability to move with increasing skill and ease.

Space stations

What you need
Hoop (or similar) for each child.

What to do
In a large, clear area, scatter hoops around the floor, one for each child. If no hoops are available, chalk out or tape circles onto the floor, or make skipping ropes or lengths of string into circles.

Begin by having the children run and find a 'space' of their own. The hoop will form the boundary of their space. Challenge the children to fill their space, making themselves as large as possible while standing up and then while sitting down. Then ask if they can take up as little space as possible. Say the following rhyme while the children carry out the actions:

> Look at me, I'm really big,
> I'm stretching tall and wide,
> But when I'm tired of being big,
> I can curl up small and hide.

Explain to the children that when they hear you say, 'Space stations', they should run to a different hoop and change spaces with another child. Repeat the rhyme and suggest other ways for the children to fill their space, such as becoming as narrow, round or flat as they can.

Support and extension
Let younger children become familiar with making big and small shapes within their space at first. Encourage older children to build up a sequence of movements they can repeat, which involve them stepping inside and outside their space.

Further ideas
■ Ask the children to stand outside their space station and to put different parts of their body into their space. See if they can put one knee into the hoop, or four fingers, or two elbows, while the rest of their body remains outside the space.
■ Invite the children to get into groups of three and share a space station. When the leader calls 'Space station', the children make three different shapes within the hoop, such as standing, sitting and lying down.

LEARNING OBJECTIVES
STEPPING STONE
Move spontaneously within available space.
EARLY LEARNING GOAL
Move with confidence, imagination and in safety. (PD)

GROUP SIZE
12 children.

HOME LINKS
Ask parents and carers to make a space station at home and encourage their child to dance within and around it.

Choose a partner

What you need
Tape recorder or CD player; music; selection of objects.

What to do
Collect a variety of readily available objects, such as soft toys, floaty scarves, cushions, umbrellas, handbags, feather dusters or brooms from the role-play area. Place the objects in the centre of the room and play some music for the children to dance to.

Let the children select an object from the collection and encourage them to dance with their 'partner'. Ask the children if they can dance with their partner 'over' their head, 'behind' them, to the 'side' or 'in front' of them. Can they dance with their partner 'between' their knees?

Every time the music stops, have the children exchange their partner with another child. Ask the dancers to think about how they dance differently depending upon the particular object they have as a partner. Are some partners easier to dance with than others?

Ask the children to think of other positions to hold their partners during their dance, such as 'under' their arm, 'around' their neck or 'on' their head. Encourage them to be creative.

Let the dancers take turns, in small groups of three or four, to show their dances to the rest of the children.

Support and extension
Let younger children dance with objects that are easy to hold, such as scarves or a teddy bear. Older children can try dancing with hoops or getting into twos and dancing with a large blanket.

Further ideas
■ Read 'Floppy Fiona' on the photocopiable sheet on page 67. Let the children form pairs and carry out the actions as described whenever there is a pause, taking turns to be the rag doll and the teddy bear.
■ Let the children take turns to place small toys 'inside', 'outside', 'on top of', 'behind' or 'in front of' a box placed on the floor.
■ Turn a table upside down and let the children play on the bottom of it, or tape paper to the underside of the table and encourage the children to draw upside down while lying on their backs.

Muscle power

What you need
Just the children.

What to do
Talk to the children about how their muscles can be used to push and pull. Suggest that they crouch down on the floor and use their leg muscles to push themselves upright.

Invite the children to find a partner. Have them stand facing each other holding their partner's hands. Encourage them to gently push their partner's hands away from them and then pull them back again. Ask their partner to do the same. See if they can feel the muscles in their arms working.

Now see if one of the children can make a 'butterfly'. To do this they must stand still with their arms straight down by their sides with their partner standing behind them. They then try and raise their arms outwards and up like butterfly wings, while their partner tries to prevent them by holding their arms down by their sides. Emphasise the pushing and pulling movements in their arm muscles.

Ask the first child to stand holding their arms above their head. Their partner gently tries to push them down to the sides. Next ask the first child to stand with their fists together in front of them while their partner tries to pull them apart. Then let their partner try to push them together while they try to hold them in position. Have the children change places and repeat the activities.

Support and extension
Allow younger children to concentrate on the pushing and pulling aspect of the activity, keeping the movements simple. Older children can experiment with ways of using their leg muscles to push and pull.

Further idea
■ Ask the children to make a collection of toys that need to be pulled (pull-alongs, trolleys) and toys that they must push along (toy cars, prams). Display them under, 'Toys that we push' and 'Toys that we pull' labels.

LEARNING OBJECTIVES
STEPPING STONE
Observe the effects of activity on their bodies.
EARLY LEARNING GOAL
Recognise the changes that happen to their bodies when they are active. (PD)

GROUP SIZE
Ten children.

HOME LINKS
Ask parents and carers to sing 'Row, Row, Row your Boat' with their child, sitting facing each other, soles of their feet together. As they hold hands and row the boat forwards and backwards, ask parents to emphasise the pulling and pushing movement of their arm muscles.

Who's under the blanket?

What you need
One blanket; music.

What to do
Gather together a small group of children. This activity is particularly useful for children who are not familiar with each other. Let the children say their names to everyone else in the group.

Play some lively music for the children to dance to. Ensure that all of the children are happy to join in with the dancing activity. Choose one child to stand at the side of the dancers and watch them carefully. After a few moments, have this child close or cover their eyes.

Stop the music and choose another child from the dancers to lie down on the floor. Cover them with a blanket. If the child is not confident enough to hide under the heaviness or darkness of a blanket, use a lightweight sheet in a pastel shade.

Ask the 'watcher' to open their eyes. Restart the music and let the children continue with their dance. As they do so, they chant the following question together while the child under the blanket remains quiet:

Who's under the blanket?
Who can it be?
Whoever it is,
I know it's not me!

The child now has to observe the dancers carefully and try and solve the problem of which child is missing and hiding under the blanket. If they are correct, the child who hid under the blanket now has a turn to be the watcher. If not, play the game again, this time hiding a different child.

Support and extension
When playing the game with younger children, keep the group size small to enable them to learn more easily the names of the rest of the group. Older children can play with large groups of 15 or more.

Further idea
■ Introduce subtraction by placing five teddy bears on a blanket. Have the children close their eyes and then hide two, for example, underneath the blanket. When the children open their eyes, ask them to tell you how many teddy bears are missing.

Body bumps

What you need
Tape recorder or CD player; music.

What to do
Choose music with a strong beat for this dancing activity, or have an adult beat out a rhythm on a drum.

Ask the children to hold hands and form a circle facing facing inwards. Play the music and encourage the group to move towards the centre of the circle in time to the beat of the music. When they reach the centre they raise their hands into the air and shout, 'Hey!' before stepping backwards, still in time to the beat, to their original places.

Now challenge the children to dance towards the centre of the circle leading with a different part of their body. They can try moving with their elbows first and when they all reach the centre they gently 'bump' their elbows together as they say, 'Hey!' and then step back to the outside of the circle.

See if the children can dance with their knees leading, or their shoulders, hips, bottoms or fingers. All the time make sure that the children keep to the rhythm of the music and gently touch the leading body parts together in the centre of the circle.

Support and extension
Give younger children just two ways to move to the centre of the circle, forwards or backwards, leading with their fingers or bottoms. Older children can extend their knowledge of body parts by suggesting other variations.

■■■■■■■■■■■■■■■■■■■■

Further ideas
■ Ask the children if they can make sounds using different parts of their bodies. How many sounds can they make using their hands (clapping, tapping hand on wrist, clicking their fingers), and how many sounds with their feet (stamping, jumping). Can they make a sound using their elbows or knees?
■ Cut out pictures of body parts from magazines and ask the children if they can identify them.
■ See if the children can point to the door, window or table using a different body part, such as their thumb, elbow, or knee.
■ Ask the children to make a certain part of their body (nose, feet, chin) the highest.

Around and around

What you need
Four to five hoops; tape recorder or CD player; music.

What to do
Ask the children to think about the shape of a circle. See if they can form a circle by using their thumb and forefinger. Now see if they can make one by curving their arms over their head with their fingers touching.

Have the children get into groups of four and make a circle by holding hands in a ring. Can they make their circle completely round?

LEARNING OBJECTIVES
STEPPING STONE
Show curiosity and observation by talking about shapes, how they are the same or why some are different.

EARLY LEARNING GOAL
Talk about, recognise and recreate simple patterns. (MD)

GROUP SIZE
16 to 20 children.

Give each of these groups a hoop and ask them to all hold it with both hands around the outside. (If no hoops are available use string or a skipping rope.) Play some music; waltzes and polkas by Strauss are excellent for this activity. Encourage the children to whirl and swirl around in circles as they dance to the music. Suggest that they are not too enthusiastic otherwise they may pull the other children in their group off their feet.

Stop the music and ask the children to make another group of four with different children, before continuing with their dance. Vary the speed of the music, so that sometimes the children are dancing slowly around their hoops and sometimes quickly.

Support and extension
Younger children may need an adult to lead them in their dance. Let older children join their hoops together to make one giant circle.

HOME LINKS
Suggest that parents and carers make circle pictures with their child by printing with paper cups, bottle caps or pastry cutters dipped in paint.

Further ideas
■ Cut circles out of coloured paper and tape them to the floor. Play some music and have the children dance around the circles. When the music stops the children must stand on one of the circles and then say what colour circle they are standing on.
■ Play musical circles by placing hoops on the ground. Play music and when the music stops the children stand inside one of the hoops. Each time the music stops, remove one of the hoops. As the hoops become more crowded, name a body part (hand, foot, elbow) to put in the hoop.

Beanbag ballet

What you need
Ten beanbags.

What to do
Provide a beanbag for each child in the group. A sock stuffed with some crumpled newspaper will suffice if no beanbags are available.

Explain to the children that as a group you are going to be trying to find as many ways as possible to move the beanbag to the other side of the room. Firstly, ask the children to find a way to move the beanbag across the room by balancing it on different parts of their body. Can they balance it on their head, elbow, foot or shoulder?

Encourage the children to think of ways to carry the beanbag, such as in the crook of their elbow, between their knees or in their armpits. Can they now find different methods to push the beanbag across the room on the floor, perhaps using their heels, nose, shoulders, fists or chin. Finally, have the children find a partner and work together to transport the beanbag, cooperating to balance or push it together.

Talk to the children about the ways they moved their beanbag and let individuals demonstrate to the rest of the group. Discuss how they might develop and improve on their ideas. Talk about the different body parts that they used to move their beanbag, using vocabulary such as wrist, palms, chin and forearm.

Support and extension
Be aware of younger children who may need help during this activity and begin with two or three suggestions if required. Older children can have races to see who can be the first to balance, carry or push their beanbag across the room.

Further ideas
■ Ask the children to throw their beanbag in the air. When the beanbag lands on the floor, call out a body part. The child picks it up and places it quickly on that part of their body.
■ Replace beanbags with other items, such as soft toys, balls or books. Are these things easier or more difficult to move than beanbags?

LEARNING OBJECTIVES
STEPPING STONE
Use increasing control over an object by touching, pushing, patting, throwing, catching or kicking it.

EARLY LEARNING GOAL
Use a range of small and large equipment. (PD)

GROUP SIZE
Ten children.

HOME LINKS
Encourage parents and carers to give their child the opportunity to balance and carry things, under supervision, in the home.

Hands up

What you need
Tape recorder or CD player; music; red marker or face-paint.

What to do
Ask the children to warm up by finding out how many ways they can move their hands. Can they waggle their wrists up and down and around, wriggle their fingers, make a fist with their left hand, point a finger on their right hand, snap their fingers, clap, wave and so on. How far up can their hands reach and how low down? Can they touch their hands behind their back?

Using face-paint or a washable marker pen, (a sticky paper red spot could also be used) make a large red dot on the children's right hand. Practise a few times by asking the children to raise their right hand (the one with the red spot) and then their left hand (the one without).

Play music and ask the children to create a dance using lots of hand movements. When you call, 'Right', the children dance with their right hand in the air, then do the same with their left hand.

At the end of the dance, have the children find a partner to shake hands with, using their right hand.

Support and extension
Tie ribbons or scarves around the right wrists of younger children to make their right hand easier to identify. Older children can participate without using any visible markers.

Further ideas
■ Complete the photocopiable sheet 'What are these hands doing?' on page 68, with the children.
■ Sew buttons onto the fingers of old pairs of gloves and let the children explore the different sounds they can make as they tap their fingers on different surfaces, such as metal, plastic, wood, fabric or cardboard. Discuss which surfaces make the best sound. Let the children use first the left glove and then the right.

On the line

What you need
Chalk (or length of string).

What to do
Make a pathway along the ground outdoors using chalk if on a hard surface, or mark it in sand or earth. If carrying out the activity indoors use a long length of string. Begin by drawing a simple straight line.

Ask the children to move along the line in small heel-to-toe steps. See if the children can then suggest different ways to move along the line. They may want to march, jump, dance, twirl, hop and so on.

Try drawing other lines, making the pathways curved, wiggly or in a zigzag pattern. Ask the children to pretend that a bird is flying overhead and that they should move along the line using a high, stretched walk or on tiptoe, as they try to catch it. Alternatively, ask the children to pretend that there is a beetle on the line and crawl or move in a low creeping walk to find it. As the children move along the pathway sing the following rhyme to the tune of 'Frère Jacques':

> *We are (marching), we are (marching),*
> *On the line, on the line.*
> *We're following the line, we're following the line,*
> *See us (march), see us (march).*

When they reach the end, encourage the children to turn around and march back again. Repeat the activity with the children walking, skipping, hopping and so on.

Support and extension
Draw two parallel lines for younger children to move between. Older children can follow more complicated lines that cross over one another.

Further ideas
■ Lay a trail of footprints, either indoors or outside, for the children to follow. Draw cat prints on paper and cut them out. Ask the children to follow the trail moving like a cat. You could also leave a trail of horse or bear prints.

■ Create an obstacle path for children to move along. Hang a blanket over a table to crawl through, place carpet squares or hoops on the floor to act as stepping stones, walk along a low bench and weave between cones.

LEARNING OBJECTIVES
STEPPING STONE
Negotiate an appropriate pathway when walking, running or using a wheelchair or other mobility aids, both indoors and outdoors.

EARLY LEARNING GOAL
Show awareness of space, of themselves and of others. (PD)

GROUP SIZE
Up to ten children.

HOME LINKS
Explain to parents and carers that you are exploring pathways and suggest that they take a different route home or to the local shop.

Hello, goodbye

What you need
Tape recorder or CD player; music.

What to do
Discuss what sort of things we do and what sort of movements we make when
we say hello or goodbye to someone.

Ask the children to find a partner and shake hands with them, bow or
curtsey to one another, wave goodbye or hug each other.

Play music for the children to dance to. Every time the music stops, ask the
children to run and find a partner. Explain that if they hear you call out, 'Hi!',
they should greet their partner. If they hear you call out, 'Bye!', they should
perform a farewell action. The children should choose different partners each
time the music stops.

To help children get to know others in their group, have them introduce
themselves to their partner when you call, 'Hi!' by saying, 'Hello, I'm (child's
name)' before carrying out the action. When you call, 'Bye!' they can say,
'Goodbye, (child's name)'.

Support and extension
Keep the groups small with younger children and encourage them to try and
learn everyone's name in the group. Have older children make up a simple
'hello and goodbye' song to the tune of a familiar nursery rhyme.

Further ideas
■ One morning, during
greeting time, encourage
the children to think
how they feel. If they are
unhappy they could dance
a 'sad dance', or dance in a
happy, angry or sleepy way.
■ Invite someone known
to the children, such as a
crossing warden, to come
in and say 'hello' to them,
introduce themselves, invite
questions and then say
'goodbye'.
■ Talk about what it means
to be friends with someone.
Friends share things, play
together, talk and listen to
each other, and friends are
special. Ask the children to
paint pictures of themselves
saying hello to their friend.

The living world

Use aspects of nature to inspire the children's imagination. These activities include the seasons and weather, trees and flowers, and animals and insects to enable the children to move and dance with inventiveness.

Under the sea

What you need
Tape recorder or CD player; music.

What to do
Discuss creatures that live in the sea with the group. Ask the children to think about how eels, sharks, octopuses, jellyfish or whales might move. Jellyfish float, eels wriggle, whales glide and dive, sharks dash, octopuses wave their arms and starfish make shapes on the floor. Encourage the children to use their imagination to create a 'fishy dance'.

Play music, such as 'Aquarium' from *Carnival of the Animals* by Saint-Saëns or the song 'Under the Sea' from the soundtrack to *The Little Mermaid*, for the children to dance to.

Divide the group in half and have one group pretending to be seaweed, swaying and waving while anchored to the bottom of the sea. The other group then performs their fishy dance, swimming in and out of the seaweed.

Half-way through the activity, on the cue, 'Fisherman!' the fish and the seaweed reverse roles.

Support and extension
Provide suggestions as to how the sea creatures might move for younger children. Let older children join together in groups of four and see if they can move like an octopus with eight arms.

Further ideas
■ Let the children fill plastic lidded containers with sand or shells to use as shakers to accompany their dance.
■ Place pictures of whales on the walls around the room. Provide the children with a pair of binoculars and let them take turns to 'whale watch'.
■ Cut out pictures or drawings of sea creatures and lay them on the floor. Lay a sheet, preferably blue, over them. Have the children stand around the edge of the sheet and pick it up, shaking it up and down to create waves. Let the children take turns to 'swim' under the sheet, pick up one of the pictures and say what it is. Invite them to place the picture on top of the sheet so that it floats on the waves. Continue until all the pictures have been retrieved from under the sea.

Silly seasons

LEARNING OBJECTIVES

STEPPING STONE
Show an awareness of change.

EARLY LEARNING GOAL
Look closely at similarities, differences, patterns and change. (KUW)

GROUP SIZE
Any size.

What you need
Just the children.

What to do
Ask the children if they know what season it is at the present time and how they know. Discuss seasonal changes and what signs to look for.

Encourage the children to create a winter dance. They could be throwing snowballs, floating like snowflakes, moving and melting like a snowman or creating a spiky, sharp, shivery Jack Frost dance. Then change to a spring dance, pretending to plant seeds, grow and stretch like a flower, rush and dash like the March wind or gambol like lambs.

Summer follows, and a summer dance may include a fluttering butterfly, a buzzing bee, paddling at the seaside or eating a giant ice cream. Children can then twirl around like autumn leaves, pretend to be a curling animal getting ready to hibernate, splash in rain puddles or create a splodgy mud dance.

Ask the children to join in with the following rhyme:

Summer, autumn, winter, spring,
I wonder what the day will bring?
Tumbling leaves or falling snow,
A shining sun or flowers that grow.
Look outside, what can you see?
Just what season will it be?

At the end of the rhyme, call out a season and ask the children to dance the appropriate dance. Mix up the seasons, if you wish, so that the children do not know which one to expect.

Support and extension
With younger children, concentrate on the current season only. Allow older children to develop their seasonal dances in a more detailed way and take turns to call out the seasons.

HOME LINKS
Encourage parents and carers to go on a walk with their child, pointing out things of seasonal interest and collecting interesting items to discuss with the rest of the group.

Further ideas
■ Collect four seasonal items, such as a seaside bucket, woollen hat, leaf or acorn, and seed packet. With the children sitting in a circle, have them pass the items around the circle as they say the above rhyme. At the end of the rhyme ask the children who are left holding the four items to say what they have and which season it represents.
■ Collect seasonal clothing. Using pictures from old calendars, sort the clothing by the season in which the children would wear it.
■ Make four large seasonal collages.

Mole in a hole

What you need
Just the children.

What to do
Discuss with the children how a mole lives under the ground. They make tunnels and, although we do not see them very often, they leave molehills to show where they have been.

Explain to the children that they are going to form a tunnel for a mole to crawl through. Ask them to stand one behind the other, with their legs apart, and their hands on the shoulders of the child in front.

Choose the child at the back of the line to be the 'mole'. Ask the mole to crawl through the tunnel formed by the children, trying not to touch anyone. Encourage the mole to keep as low and small as possible while crawling through the space, and the children forming the tunnel to keep their legs as wide as possible, making as large a space as they can.

When the mole reaches the end of the tunnel, ask 'it' to stand at the front of the line. The child now at the back becomes the next mole.

See if the children can think of different ways of making a tunnel, such as bending over and touching the ground with their hands to form an arch.

Support and extension
Keep the tunnel short for younger children to crawl through, consisting of five or six children. Encourage older children to make long, wiggly tunnels to move through and think of different ways to crawl.

■■■■■■■■■■■■■■■■

Further ideas
■ Play other 'Over and under' games, such as 'Rivers and bridges'. Have two children form a bridge while the rest of the group crawl through one after the other, head to toe, as the river. See if the children can move slowly and then faster as the river rushes by.
■ Ask the children how many things with holes they can thread on a shoelace.
■ Look at holes in clothes for arms, necks and legs, and holes in their faces (mouth, nostrils and ears).

Autumn leaves

What you need
Just the children.

What to do
Ask the children if they can mime kicking and shuffling through a pile of dry autumn leaves, throwing the leaves in the air and trying to catch them, jumping into a heap of leaves, and swirling, floating and fluttering down to the floor like a falling leaf.

Encourage all the children to join in with the following action rhyme, sung to the tune of 'Twinkle, Twinkle, Little Star':

Flutter, flutter, little leaves (children flutter their fingers)
Blowing high up in the trees. (flutter arms above head)
Autumn's here, the time has come (sway arms above head)
To leave your branches one by one.
(raise arms alternately, fluttering fingers up and down)
Red and orange, yellow and brown (wave fingers above head)
Tumbling down upon the ground. (bring fingers down to ground)

At the end of the rhyme the children can carry out their leaf dance. Tell the children that when they hear you call out, 'Fall' at the end of the dance, they should immediately fall to the ground.

Support and extension
Keep the session shorter for younger children, dancing freely to the leaf theme. Introduce the action rhyme during another session. Encourage older children to make up their own leaf song as they dance.

Further ideas
■ Cut out various leaf shapes from red, orange, yellow or brown paper, so that each child in the group can have two leaves. Staple or tape each leaf to a length of ribbon or yarn and let the children hold one in each hand as they perform their leaf dance.

■ Let the children make leaf people by glueing two or three colourful autumn leaves on to a sheet of paper. Use felt-tipped pens to add arms, legs, hands, feet and other features.

Butterflies and caterpillars

What you need
Just the children.

What to do
Explore how caterpillars change into butterflies by discussing the life cycle of a caterpillar. Explain the four stages: egg, larva (caterpillar), pupa (chrysalis) and adult butterfly.

Tell the story through a movement activity. Firstly, have the children make a small round shape as the egg. They then pretend to be caterpillars crawling on a leaf by wriggling along on their stomachs. During the chrysalis stage they roll themselves into a cocoon and lie very still for a short while before they emerge and fly around as butterflies, using their arms as wings.

Ask one child to take on the role of the caller. Tell the children that when they hear the caller say, 'Blackbird!' they should freeze in their position until the danger has passed.

Tell the children that when they hear the caller say, 'Caterpillar shuffle', they should immediately form one long caterpillar by kneeling down one behind the other, holding on to the legs of the child in front. They should then shuffle along first with their right knee and then with their left.

Continue with the game, letting the children take turns to act as the caller.

Support and extension
When carrying out the caterpillar shuffle, let younger children simply make a caterpillar by standing in a line, holding on to each other's waists. Older children can be given instructions to 'shuffle towards the window' or 'through the door'.

Further ideas
■ Make sequence cards of the life cycle of a caterpillar and let the children place them in the correct order.
■ Create large butterfly pictures to hang from the ceiling. Have the children drop blobs of different coloured paint on to one side of a sheet of paper. Carefully fold the paper in half and press down. Open the paper and when the paint has dried, cut out butterfly shapes.
■ Cut lemons in half and dip in green paint. Print caterpillar pictures by pressing the lemons on to paper, slightly overlapping the circles.
■ Make butterflies by taping paper wings to an inflated balloon and display them from the ceiling.

LEARNING OBJECTIVES
STEPPING STONE
Show curiosity and interest by facial expression, movement or sound.

EARLY LEARNING GOAL
Investigate objects and materials by using all of their senses as appropriate. (KUW)

GROUP SIZE
Ten to 20 children.

HOME LINKS
Show parents and carers how their child can make a butterfly picture at home by using felt-tipped pens on a slightly damp paper towel and folding it in half.

Swirling snow

LEARNING OBJECTIVES

STEPPING STONE
Have a sense of belonging.

EARLY LEARNING GOAL
Have a developing awareness of their own needs, views and feelings and be sensitive to the needs, views and feelings of others. (PSED)

■ ■ ■ ■ ■ ■ ■ ■ ■

GROUP SIZE
15 to 20 children.

■ ■ ■ ■ ■ ■ ■ ■

What you need
Tape recorder or CD player; music.

What to do
Discuss snowflakes and explain to the children that they are made of tiny drops of frozen water, each one with its own different design. No snowflake is like any other. Emphasise that the children are like the snowflakes – they are all different too. Observe how snowflakes float, curl and swirl softly when falling to the ground.

Play suitable music, such as an extract from *The Snowman* by Raymond Briggs (music by Howard Blake). Ask the children to create a free-flow snowflake dance around the room.

Encourage the children to join in and sing a snowflake song to the tune of 'Twinkle, Twinkle, Little Star' as they dance:

> *Snowflakes, snowflakes, all around,*
> *Snowflakes swirling to the ground.*
> *Snowflakes whirling in the air,*
> *Snowflakes, snowflakes, everywhere.*
> *Sparkling white and dancing free,*
> *Each one special – just like me!*

As the children end on, 'Just like me', ask them to freeze in position. Select one of the children to choose something special about themselves and share it with the rest of the group.

Support and extension
Have an adult sing the song for younger children while they create their special snowflake dance. Older children can join with a partner to form a dancing 'snowball', or get into groups of six and form a 'snowman'.

■ ■

Further ideas
■ Make snowflakes by folding a circle of white paper into four and cutting out shapes. Thread white wool through for the children to hold as they dance their snowflake dance.
■ Make snow pictures using white materials, such as polystyrene shapes, pieces of white doily, lengths of white wool, cotton wool, rice, scraps of white fabric, or use white chalk, paint or a crayon on black paper.
■ Collect pictures of snowy scenes from old Christmas cards, photographs and winter holiday brochures. Display them along with clothes to wear on a snowy day, such as woolly hats, gloves and mittens, scarves, warm boots and quilted jackets.

HOME LINKS
Ask parents and carers if they have a photograph of their child in a winter scene that they could bring in to share with the rest of the group.

■ ■ ■ ■ ■ ■ ■

Stormy seas

What you need
Musical instruments (drum, cymbals and maracas).

What to do
Encourage the children to respond to the sounds of musical instruments in a dance activity that represents a storm at sea. Have an adult play maracas (or make a rainstick by sealing a small amount of rice in a cardboard tube and turning it over and over) and ask the children to create a rain dance, fluttering their arms and fingers down from the sky.

Crash the cymbals (or use saucepan lids) and let the children respond to the lightning sound with a jumpy, jerky, zigzag dance. Bang a drum (or beat an upturned tin with a wooden spoon) to represent thunder and encourage the children to create a big, heavy, rolling thunder dance.

Create a storm sequence, beginning with thunder, then lightning and finally rain, before fading away. The children will respond to the musical sounds by performing their rain, thunder or lightning dance.

See if the children can pretend they are the waves on the sea. Have an adult play a drum and begin with a calm sea, with the children making small arm movements. As the instrument gets faster and louder, see if the children can create bigger waves and finally huge waves, by moving their arms and bodies in larger and faster actions. As the drum slows down and fades away, the waves die down before becoming a calm sea.

Support and extension
Keep the sequences short and simple for younger children. Encourage fast responses from older children by rapidly changing the instruments. Let older children take turns to play the instruments.

Further idea
■ Cut five dark storm-cloud shapes out of paper. Number the clouds from 1 to 5 and place them on the floor. Cut 15 raindrop shapes from silver foil. Let the children take turns to identify the number on the clouds and place the correct number of raindrops underneath them.

LEARNING OBJECTIVES
STEPPING STONE
Respond to sound with body movement.

EARLY LEARNING GOAL
Recognise and explore how sounds can be changed, sing simple songs from memory, recognise repeated sounds and sound patterns and match movements to music. (CD)

GROUP SIZE
Any size.

HOME LINKS
Ask parents and carers to let their child recreate their storm music and dancing at home using kitchen utensils such as saucepan lids, tins, and rice in a tray to represent the rain.

Let's fly

What you need
Lightweight scarves; tape recorder or CD player; suitable music.

What to do
Begin by asking the children to think of as many things as they can that are able to fly. If they struggle, provide them with some suggestions, such as how do ladybirds move around? Give each child a lightweight, floaty scarf and encourage them to create a 'flying dance', using their scarf to represent wings, capes and so on. The children can pretend to be a superhero, ghost, fairy, aeroplane, bird, insect, bat or butterfly.

Provide suitable music, such as Stravinsky's *Firebird* to dance to, and encourage the children to investigate different movements through the air. Introduce words such as 'fluttering', 'flapping', 'soaring', 'swooping' and 'gliding'.

Have the children sit on the floor while an adult calls out the names of animals or objects. Tell the children that whenever the adult calls out something that can fly, they should jump up and perform a short flying dance around the room.

When the leader mentions an object that cannot fly, the children should remain sitting quietly on the floor.

Support and extension
Use a simple vocabulary with younger children. Introduce a more varied vocabulary with older children, such as saying 'robin' instead of 'bird' and 'mosquito' instead of 'insect'.

Further ideas
■ Complete the photocopiable sheet 'Can you fly?' on page 69.
■ Play a game called 'Bluebirds'. The practitioner calls out the following actions and the children respond accordingly: 'Fly' – the children find a partner and, holding hands, flap their free arm as a wing and fly together around the room. 'Tweet' – the children use their hands to make the motion of a beak opening to their partner. 'Nest' – the children squat on the floor as if sitting on a nest. 'CAT!' – the children flap their wings and fly around the room to find another partner. Begin the game again.

Dancing daisies

What you need
Tape recorder or CD player; suitable music.

What to do
Talk about daisies with the children, discussing their colour and shape. Explain that at night-time a daisy closes its petals and then opens them again in the morning. Point out how this is similar to the children when they go to sleep.

Ask the children to imagine that they are daisies. Begin by having the children stand still, keeping their arms down by their sides. It is morning and the daisies are waking up. The children slowly stretch their arms up above their head and then stretch out their fingers right to the fingertips as they reach for the sun.

Once the daisy is fully open, play suitable music and encourage the children to make a 'daisy dance' around the room as they enjoy the sun and are blown gently in the wind. As night falls, have the children come to a halt and close their petals by slowly curling their fingers into a fist, drawing their arms down to their sides and lowering their heads.

Tell the children that if, at any time during the daisy dance, they hear you call, 'Daisy chain', they should quickly form a circle and hold hands to make a daisy chain. They should then dance around in a circle, before continuing with their own daisy dance.

Support and extension
With younger children, work with small groups, providing support and suggestions for movements if necessary. Ask older children to form groups of four, six or eight when making their daisy chains.

Further ideas
■ Provide some real daisies for the children to examine closely with a magnifying glass. Note the shape of the leaves and the petals. Make daisy prints on green paper using circles in yellow for the centres and white ovals for the petals.

■ Make each child a daisy number chain by cutting out ten daisy shapes and writing the numbers 1 to 10 in the centre. Let the children place their daisies in the correct numerical order.

■ Make a giant daisy from paper and ask the children to think of other words beginning with the letter 'd' to write on each petal, such as 'dog', 'duck' and 'dark'.

LEARNING OBJECTIVES
STEPPING STONE
Make constructions, collages, paintings, drawings and dances.

EARLY LEARNING GOAL
Explore colour, texture, shape, form and space in two or three dimensions. (CD)

GROUP SIZE
Eight or more children.

HOME LINKS
Let the children take home their daisy number chains and show their families how they can place the daisies in the correct numerical order.

Tall trees

What you need
The photocopiable sheet 'The trees are growing tall' on page 70.

What to do
Ask the children to imagine that they are a tree – tall and strong. Can they stand like a tree, with their feet anchored in the ground like roots and their arms, like branches, reaching into the sky?

Ask the children to think about how a tree moves in the wind. Encourage the children to move from their waist upwards, keeping their legs straight and still like a tree trunk. Use words such as 'twist', 'turn', 'bend', 'sway', 'wave', 'tremble' and 'shake'.

Have the children place themselves around the room like trees in a wood. Choose one child to act as the wind. Ask this child to run through and around the trees, making wind noises, ranging from a soft whooshing to a loud roaring. Tell the children that as the wind passes them by, they should bend and sway according to its strength.

Tell the children that when they hear you say, 'Ssshhhhh', the wind should stop and change places with the nearest tree, who then becomes the wind. Sing together the action rhyme 'The trees are growing tall'.

Support and extension
Have an adult take the part of the wind for younger children. Ask older children to imagine they are a certain type of tree, standing with feet apart for a sturdy oak, with trailing branches for a willow, or spiky arms and fingers for a fir tree, and so on.

Further ideas
■ Collect a variety of items made from wood and plastic. Let the children sort the objects into two groups.
■ Have a 'tree tasting' session. Provide foods that grow on trees, such as apples, pears, bananas, oranges, olives, figs and chocolate (cacao tree) and let the children taste a small piece of each.
■ Cut a large tree out of paper and hang it on the wall. Cut 20 leaves from green paper and put a small amount of Blu-Tack on the back of each one. Have the children take turns putting a different number of leaves on the tree.

Let's pretend

Most children enjoy games that involve pretending, and the activities in this chapter should help gain the children's interest and full participation. Be ready to offer support to children where necessary and remember to encourage and praise each child in your group.

Washday

What to do

Explain to the children that you are going to create a 'washday dance'. Ask them to imagine that they are clothes in a washing machine.

Invite the group to think about what happens to the clothes, and to use their imagination to tumble around when washing and then spin themselves dry. When they hang themselves out on the line to dry, have the whole group join hands to make a long washing line and flap and blow in the wind.

Ask the children to imagine they are soap bubbles, floating around the room on tiptoe and gently bumping into each other. As the children move, sing the following bubble song to the tune of 'I Hear Thunder'. When the children say the word, 'Pop', they should pretend to burst and fall to the floor.

Bubbles, bubbles,
Bubbles, bubbles,
Everywhere,
Everywhere,
Floating in the air,
Floating in the air,
Pop, pop, pop!
POP, POP, POP!

Support and extension

Simplify the activity for younger children by concentrating on moving like bubbles and singing the rhyme. Encourage older children to create a sequence of movements to represent washday, which they are able to repeat.

■ ■

Further ideas

■ Blow commercially-bought bubble solution, either indoors or outdoors, play soft, gentle music, such as 'Greensleeves' by Vaughan Williams, and have the children dance on tiptoe as they try and catch the bubbles.
■ Play a laundry game by tying a clothes line or skipping rope low enough for the children. Divide the players into two teams and provide each child with an item of clothing. Place enough clothes pegs (two per player) by the clothes line. On a signal, the first child in each team runs to the clothes line, takes two pegs, and hangs up their item of clothing. They then run back to their team and the next player goes. See which team can peg out their washing the fastest.

LEARNING OBJECTIVES
STEPPING STONE
Develop a repertoire of actions by putting a sequence of movements together.
EARLY LEARNING GOAL
Use their imagination in art and design, music, dance, imaginative and role-play and stories. (CD)

GROUP SIZE
15 to 20 children.

HOME LINKS
Ask parents and carers to let children make bubbles to play with, using a bowl of warm water and plenty of washing-up liquid.

Come to the circus

What you need

Length of rope.

What to do

Discuss with the children the different performers they may see in the circus, such as clowns, tightrope walkers, jugglers, acrobats, a marching band and circus horses. Ask the children to think about what these performers do and how they move.

Place a rope or length of string on the floor and encourage them to balance along it carefully, one foot in front of the other, as if on a tightrope. Challenge the children to balance on one leg on the tightrope.

See if the children can create a funny clown dance to make each other laugh. Encourage any children juggling to pretend to juggle while balancing on different parts of their body (back, bottom, knees, on one leg and so on). Those doing acrobatics can explore different ways to roll (forward roll, rolling sideways to one side and then to the other, rolling curled up in a ball).

The children can pretend to be circus horses by prancing around the room, one behind the other, with knees high. Have an adult act as a 'ringmaster' and introduce the circus acts.

Support and extension

Limit the circus activities to one or two per session with younger children. Encourage older children to think of other activities carried out by acrobats, clowns and jugglers and let them take turns to act as the ringmaster.

Further ideas

■ Make clown hats using a circular piece of card folded into a conical shape and decorating it with glitter. Use face-paints to make clown faces. Cut out extra large clown shoes from card and tape them to the bottom of the children's shoes. Play suitable music for the children to carry out their clown dance.

■ Show the children how to be a circus horse carrying a bareback rider. When the children are on their hands and knees, place a soft toy or teddy bear on their back. They then have to crawl around the room without the rider falling off.

Fireworks

What you need
A selection of musical instruments.

What to do
As Bonfire Night draws near, discuss different types of fireworks with the children, such as bangers, sparklers, rockets and Catherine wheels. Emphasise the danger of fireworks to the children, the importance of never handling fireworks themselves, and always making sure an adult is supervising the lighting.

Encourage the children to think of different movements to represent each firework. For example, they can crouch down, jump up high and then crouch again every time a banger goes off. Rockets can be portrayed by jumping up as high as they can, arms reaching above their head, before 'exploding'. Children can whirl and spin around quickly like a whizzing Catherine wheel, or shoot their arms and legs out in jerky, sharp movements like a sparkler.

Encourage the children to use their imagination when imitating the fireworks and then put together a sequence of movements for a 'firework dance'. As they do so help them to become aware of the patterns they are making around the room, straight, curved, twisting or zigzagging.

Let the children accompany their dance using musical instruments. Cymbals, shakers, woodblocks, guiros and kazoos are suitable instruments for representing fireworks.

Support and extension
Let younger children follow an older or more capable child as they create their dance. Play an 'All change' game with older children where an adult calls out the name of a firework and the children respond as quickly as they can with that particular firework's dance.

Further ideas
■ Make firework pictures using thick fluorescent paint in bright red, yellow and orange, or a collage using materials such as foil, sequins, cellophane, tinsel, glitter and transparent, brightly-coloured sweet wrappers.
■ Give each child a beanbag to place on the floor in a space. Have the children run around their beanbag until the leader shouts, 'Bang!' The children then 'explode' in a straight direction until the leader shouts, 'Stop!' They then return to their beanbag.

LEARNING OBJECTIVES
STEPPING STONE
Develop a repertoire of actions by putting a sequence of movements together.

EARLY LEARNING GOAL
Use their imagination in art and design, music, dance, imaginative and role play and stories. (CD)

GROUP SIZE
Any size.

HOME LINKS
Invite parents and carers to join you in lighting sparklers with the children on Bonfire Night. Let children perform their fireworks dance.

Flamenco

What you need
Tape recorder or CD player; suitable Spanish flamenco music; castanets; scarves.

What to do
Introduce dance from other countries to the children, beginning with the flamenco, the traditional dance of Spain.

Discuss with the children how traditional Spanish dancers move. This involves stamping feet, clapping hands and lots of clicking of toes and heels with hands held over their head. They also like wiggling their fingers in the air and flicking their wrists.

Encourage the children to be particularly aware of body parts such as heels, toes, elbows, wrists and chins. Let them explore these movements freely.

Tie scarves around the waists of the girls to represent a Spanish dress. Play some fast, rousing, flamenco guitar music for the children to create their Spanish dance to. The children can accompany their dance with plenty of 'Olés'.

Support and extension
Provide demonstrations to help younger children, let them join in when they are ready. Encourage older children to use castanets while dancing.

Further ideas
■ Dance the tarantella from Italy by providing each child with a tambourine. Form a circle facing the centre, take eight steps to the right, then eight steps to the left. Taking small skipping steps, children meet in the centre of the circle, raising their tambourines and banging them high over their heads. They then step back to the outer circle, bang their tambourines again, then repeat the sequence.

■ Introduce the Hora, a traditional dance from Israel. Dancers form a circle, holding the elbows or shoulders of the child on either side of them. Sway three times to the right, then to the left. Move slowly around in a circle, gradually moving faster and faster. Stop and move to the centre of the circle, raise hands high, then return to the outside of the circle. Continue the sequence.

■ Make hula skirts out of strips of crêpe paper. Play suitable Hawaiian music and let the children dance, using their hips and arms to sway to the rhythm.

■ Place a large decorated hat on the floor, play lively Mexican music and let the children create a 'Mexican hat dance'.

Cowboy capers

What you need
Tape recorder or CD player; suitable music.

What to do
Encourage the children to pretend they are cowboys on horses, galloping around the room with knees high in a 'horse dance', holding their imaginary reins in front of them.

Select some music that is fast and exciting, such as the *William Tell* Overture by Rossini. As the children gallop around to the music, emphasise the importance of carefully looking where they are going to avoid bumping into each other.

When the children can move around the space at speed in a controlled manner, see if they can make patterns on the floor during their dance. With the children one behind the other, cross the floor diagonally from one corner to the other or make a figure of eight pattern. Another variation is to make a serpentine path down the room, moving backwards and forwards from one side of the room to the other.

Have an adult in the lead until the children are familiar with the movements. Challenge the group to think of other patterns they could include in their dance.

Support and extension
Let younger children simply enjoy galloping around as cowboys on their pretend horses. With older children try dividing the group into two, moving in opposite directions as they pass each other, or form two circles which gallop in opposite directions.

Further ideas
■ Provide wide-brimmed hats as cowboy hats for the children to wear, along with waistcoats and squares of coloured material as bandannas.
■ Cut 12 cowboy-hat shapes out of coloured paper and divide into pairs. Colour the bands on each pair differently, using stripes, spots, zigzag patterns and so on. Mix up the hats and let the children take turns to find the matching pairs.
■ Sing traditional rhymes, such as 'Ride a Cock Horse', and encourage the children to slap their thighs to represent the sound of horses galloping. See if the children can think of any other rhymes which feature horses.

LEARNING OBJECTIVES
STEPPING STONE
Enjoy joining in with dancing and ring games.

EARLY LEARNING GOAL
Recognise and explore how sounds can be changed, sing simple songs from memory, recognise repeated sounds and sound patterns and match movements to music. (CD)

GROUP SIZE
Ten or more children.

HOME LINKS
Ask parents and carers to use everyday items in the home to make the 'clip-clop' noises of hooves as the children gallop around on their horses.

Monster mash

What you need
Just the children.

What to do
Ask the children to imagine a friendly monster and to think about how a monster might move, such as stomping, plodding, shuffling, scuttling and creeping. Have the children create a 'friendly monster dance'. Think of a name for their imaginary monster.

Discuss how monsters have feelings too. Sing the following song to the tune of 'What Shall We Do With the Drunken Sailor?' and encourage the children to dance a monster dance, showing the different emotions suggested by the words in the song:

What shall we do with the angry monster?
What shall we do with the angry monster?
What shall we do with the angry monster?
Early in the morning.
Let him stamp and stomp until he's happy, (and so on).

What shall we do with the frightened monster? (and so on).
Give him a hug until he's better, (and so on).

What shall we do with the sad old monster? (and so on).
Tickle him all over until he laughs, (and so on).

What shall we do with the noisy monster? (and so on).
Let him shout and roar until he's quiet, (and so on).

Talk about how we all feel like the monster in the song at times. Ask the children what they do to feel better.

Support and extension
Emphasise to younger children, who may be apprehensive, that it is a friendly monster and allow them to watch if necessary before taking part. Older children could suggest other feelings and emotions the monster may have, such as sleepy, hungry or surprised, and incorporate these into the song.

Further ideas
■ Give each child a copy of the photocopiable sheet 'Monster moods' on page 72 and let them identify the feelings expressed by the monsters and colour in the pictures.
■ Create monster masks using egg-box trays. Round off the edges and cut out holes for the eyes and mouth. Add large teeth and eyebrows. Decorate with fur, feathers, pipe-cleaners, straw, twigs and so on.
■ Make pictures of monsters using paint or collage materials, such as shiny fabric, bubble wrap, beads, cotton wool, straw and other odds and ends.

Blow, blow, pop!

What you need
Balloon.
Remember to always supervise children when playing with balloons.

What to do
Explain to the children that they are going to go on a balloon adventure. Blow up a balloon and let it go, watching as it flies across the room. Have the children take deep breaths to inflate themselves and then shoot around the room as the air rushes out of them.

Ask the children to float around the room as balloons, making themselves as round as possible, without touching any other balloons.

Have all the children form a giant balloon by making a tight circle, holding hands. When the leader says, 'Blow', everyone blows hard into the middle of the circle, and then takes a step backwards as the balloon inflates.

The leader continues to say, 'Blow', with everyone taking a step backwards, until the balloon is fully inflated and cannot get any bigger without the children breaking contact. When the leader says, 'POP!' everyone falls to the ground as the balloon bursts.

Support and extension
Place younger children near an adult to provide support as necessary as they blow up the imaginary giant balloon. Older children can develop their balloon adventure by pretending to be blowing one on a windy day, getting it caught in a tree and watching it burst.

■■■■■■■■■■■■■

Further ideas
■ Make balloon prints by putting three different colours of paint into separate trays. Partially blow up three balloons that match each paint colour and place them in the paint. Then have the children press them gently on to a piece of paper and repeat with the balloons in other colours.

■ Make a balloon number line by blowing up ten balloons and writing large numbers 1 to 10 on them using a black marker pen. Attach string to the balloons and ask the children to place them in numerical order, and then tie them to a fence outdoors.

LEARNING OBJECTIVES
STEPPING STONE
Use their bodies to explore texture and space.

EARLY LEARNING GOAL
Explore colour, texture, shape, form and space in two or three dimensions. (CD)

GROUP SIZE
Six to ten children.

HOME LINKS
Write each child's name on a balloon-shaped piece of card and attach a short length of yarn to the bottom. Let the children take their balloon name cards home and share their balloon dance with their families.

Noah's Ark

What you need

Tape (or chalk); the photocopiable sheet 'Noah and the big rain' on page 73.

What to do

Read the story 'Noah and the big rain' to the children, without the pauses.

Make an ark-shaped outline on the ground using tape, or use chalk if outdoors. Choose one boy and one girl to act as Mr and Mrs Noah.

Have the rest of the children find a partner. Encourage each pair of children to discuss between themselves which animals they want to represent. Emphasise the need to listen to what their partner suggests as well as initiating ideas of their own. Once they have chosen their animal, they must now decide how that animal will move. Suggest a range of animal movements, such as bears walking on all fours with stiff arms and legs; frogs squatting, hands on floor and then jumping; ducks waddling with hands holding ankles, and snakes wriggling along on their tummies.

One pair at a time, the children approach Mr and Mrs Noah at the entrance to the Ark and ask:

Oh, Mr Noah please let us on your Ark.
It's raining and cold and it's getting very dark.

Mr Noah replies:
Of course I will, but answer me do,
Exactly what kind of animal are you?

The children move like the animal they have decided upon and Mr and Mrs Noah decide what they are. If they are correct the animals enter the Ark and sit down. Continue until all the children are on the Ark before the rain comes.

Support and extension

For younger children, be prepared to provide assistance when deciding upon an animal and how it moves. Encourage older children to explore more complex animal movements, such as a seal, dragging the body and legs forward using straight arms.

Further idea

■ Reread the story of 'Noah and the big rain', this time encouraging the children to use their imagination to make the appropriate movements during the story whenever there is a pause.

Rain dance

What you need
Drum.

What to do
Explain to the children how the Native Americans would dance to ask the Rain God to send them rain so that their crops would grow. Have the children make a circle and stamp around to the count of four beats, with the children chanting, 'one, two, three, four'.

When the children are confident moving in rhythm to the count of four, encourage them to emphasise the first beat with a stronger stamp: **one**, two, three, four. **One**, two, three, four. Ask an adult to keep time to the rhythm by beating a drum. After a while, stop and dance around the circle in the opposite direction.

Introduce arm movements, inviting the children to extend their arms upwards and outwards on the first stronger beat, looking up towards the sky as if asking for rain, then lowering them and holding them across their chest for the second, third and fourth beat.

Try making the beat of the drum slower and faster and ask the children to respond accordingly. Play a 'Freeze' game where all the children stop and stand still when the drum beat stops, before continuing the rain dance again.

Support and extension
Let younger children enjoy dancing around to the rhythm of the drum without including the beats of four. Make up more complex rhythms for older children to copy and let them take turns to play the drum to keep the beat.

LEARNING OBJECTIVES
STEPPING STONE
Begin to move rhythmically.

EARLY LEARNING GOAL
Recognise and explore how sounds can be changed, sing simple songs from memory, recognise repeated sounds and sound patterns and match movements to music. (CD)

GROUP SIZE
Any size.

Further ideas
■ Make ankle bells for each child by sewing jingle bells on to lengths of elastic. Sew the ends of the elastic together to form bands that fit around their ankles.
■ Make Native American headdresses by cutting strips of coloured card to make headbands to fit the children's heads. Staple real or paper feathers to the headband.
■ Cut out a cloud shape from grey card and glue on cotton wool. Cut thin strips of aluminium foil and tape them to the bottom of the cloud. Make a handle from string for the children to hold as they dance.

HOME LINKS
Let the children take home their Native American headdresses and show their rain dance to their families.

All aboard

What you need
Just the children.

What to do
Have an adult act as the engine of a train and decide upon places around the room that will be 'stations'. These could be shown by using features, such as a window or door, or by marking the station with a chair or written sign.

Ask the children to choose a station and wait there until the train arrives. As the engine moves around the stations, the children join the train by standing one behind the other and placing their hands on the shoulder of the child in front. The train continues around the room until the children are all aboard.

As the train moves between the stations have the leader choose an action for all those children already on the train to carry out. When the leader calls, 'All aboard!' as the train is about to leave the station, this acts as a signal for the next action to begin. As well as choosing actions, such as hopping, jumping, sliding, creeping, stamping and so on, have the leader choose a direction in which to move (forwards, sideways or backwards).

When the children are familiar with the activity, let them choose if they want to get off the train at a station and then get aboard when the train comes around again. As the children move around on the train, chant the following rhyme:

Here comes the train with its wheels so round,
Hopping, hopping, into town.
In the sun, or in the rain,
The wheels go round on the little red train.

Here comes the train with its wheels so round,
Stamping, stamping, into town. (and so on)

Support and extension
Keep the actions simple with younger children, such as stamping forwards or walking backwards, and encourage them to keep contact with each other when forming the train. Let older children take turns acting as the engine of the train and decide which actions to perform.

Further idea
■ Make a large frieze of a train and pin it to a wall. Have the children paint pictures of themselves, cut them out and place them in the windows of the train.

Playing games

These activities should be as much fun as possible for the children so that they enjoy playing them as they learn. Take care to ensure a safe environment for the children to move in and remind the children to avoid bumping into others as they run or dance.

Traffic lights

What you need
Just the children.

What to do
Discuss the importance of traffic lights with the group. Reinforce the fact that when the lights are on green, traffic is allowed to move. When the lights turn to amber, traffic must get ready to stop and when the lights are on red, traffic must stop.

Before the game commences, ask the children to choose a partner, then jumble themselves up and find a space on their own to stand in. Explain to the children that they are going to play a 'Change' game. Have an adult call out the following commands while the children carry out the appropriate actions:

Green: *Everyone runs around pretending to drive a car*
Amber: *Everyone walks around*
Red: *Everyone immediately stands still*
Bridge: *All the children find their partner, one of them forms a bridge by bending over and placing their hands on the floor while the other drives underneath*
Police: *Everyone immediately falls to the floor.*

This can be made into a 'Knockout' game. The last player, or pair, to carry out the action called, or to carry out the incorrect action, has to go into the 'garage' until the next game.

Support and extension
Give younger children a few minutes doing each action before calling out the change, introducing the 'bridge' option when they are familiar with the game. Make the changes short and snappy with older children to encourage quick responses. Challenge them to think of different ways to form a bridge and let them take turns to act as the caller.

Further idea
■ Have a 'Transport day' and invite the children to bring in a transportation toy, labelled with their name. Let the children sort and categorise the toys and encourage sharing.

LEARNING OBJECTIVES
STEPPING STONE
Can stop.

EARLY LEARNING GOAL
Move with confidence, imagination and in safety. (PD)

GROUP SIZE
Ten to 15 children.

HOME LINKS
Explain to parents and carers that you have been talking about traffic lights. Ask them to point out the different colours and their meaning when driving, or on a pedestrian crossing.

Pick and pass

**LEARNING
OBJECTIVES**
STEPPING STONE
Manipulate materials
and objects by
picking up, releasing,
arranging, threading
and posting them.

**EARLY LEARNING
GOAL**
Move with control
and coordination.
(PD)

GROUP SIZE
18 children.

What you need
Two plastic bowls; 18 small unbreakable objects.

What to do
Divide the group into two teams and have the teams sit facing each other in a row, about two metres apart. Place nine of the small objects (these could include a small ball of wool, a piece of LEGO, a toy car or a marble) by the first child in each team. Beside the last child in the team, place a plastic bowl.

Walk down the line of one team, alternately naming each child 'spoon' and 'plate', making sure to begin and end with a 'spoon'. Then do the same with the other team. All the children who are 'plates' sit with their hands cupped in front of them.

When you say, 'Go!', the first 'spoon' picks up one of the objects and places it on the 'plate' of the child sitting next to them. The second 'spoon' then picks up the object from the 'plate' and places it on the 'plate' of the child sitting on their other side, and so on, until the object reaches the end of the line. The last 'spoon' in the team takes the object and puts it in the bowl on the floor next to them.

The child at the beginning of the line then chooses another object and passes it down the line in the same way. See which team can get all their objects to the end of the line and into their bowl first. Change the children around so that those who were 'spoons' are now 'plates'. If any child drops the object at any time, it has to go back to the beginning of the line and start again.

Support and extension
Begin with slightly larger objects when playing the game with younger children. See if older children can play with one hand behind their back or with their eyes closed.

HOME LINKS
Ask parents and
carers to let their
child clip clothes
pegs around the
edge of a plate or
hang dolls clothes
from a low washing
line.

Further idea
■ Collect an assortment of small items, such as buttons, counters, or marbles, and see how quickly children can pick them up and place them in separate sections of an egg-box or ice-cube tray.

Busy bees

What you need
Just the children.

What to do
Encourage the children to take part in a 'bee dance' with a partner. This is a good opportunity for any children new to the group to meet and interact with the other children.

You will need an even number of children for this activity, or include an adult. Ask the children to find a partner. Have an adult call out the following actions while the children carry them out in their pairs:

Back bees:	*Children stand back to back*
Feet bees:	*Children sit facing each other, legs outstretched in front of them, with their feet touching*
Hand bees:	*Children, with arms outstretched, place the palms of their hands flat against those of their partner*
Jump bees:	*Children hold hands with their partner and jump up and down*
Spin bees:	*Children hold hands with their partner and twirl around.*

When the adult calls, 'Busy bees', the group make a buzzing noise and dance around as bees, hands flapping quickly to represent wings, as they 'fly' to find a different partner. Continue with the game for as long as required.

Support and extension
Pair very young children with an adult. For older children, play the game with an odd number of children and have the child without a partner act as the leader. Call them the 'queen bee'.

Further ideas
■ Give each child a copy of the photocopiable sheet 'Buzzing bees' on page 74 for the children to complete.
■ Draw and cut out a beehive shape and glue it to the front of a box. Make a slit in the top. Cut out bee shapes from card and on each one glue either a picture of something beginning with 'b' or another letter. Only things beginning with 'b' can go in the box. The children take turns to choose a bee and decide if it can be posted in the beehive.
■ Make bees from yellow balloons. Draw stripes around the balloons with black marker pens and add eyes and a mouth. Tie string to the balloons and let the children 'buzz' them around the room.

LEARNING OBJECTIVES
STEPPING STONE
Relate and make attachments to members of their group.

EARLY LEARNING GOAL
Form good relationships with adults and peers. (PSED)

GROUP SIZE
Ten or more children.

HOME LINKS
Encourage parents and carers to take part in simple partner games with their child.

Grumpy old bear

What you need
Chalk or tape; small chair.

What to do
Play a 'Chasing' game, either indoors or outside. Mark out boundaries for the game using chalk or tape. You will need a long, straight line at one end of the playing area, behind which is a 'safe' area. At the other end mark out a small circle to represent the bear's den. Place a chair in the centre of the circle.

Choose a child to play the part of the grumpy old bear and to sit on the chair in the bear's den. All the rest of the children line up along the 'safe' line. The children move forwards from the line towards the bear, chanting as they do so:

> *Grumpy old bear*
> *Sitting in a chair,*
> *Try and catch me*
> *If you dare!*

At the end of the chant the bear asks, 'Whose children are you?' and the children reply, 'Not yours!' When the bear, instead of asking whose children they are, says, 'You're MY children!', he leaves his den and chases them.

The children scatter and run as fast as they can back to the 'safe' line. As the children run for home, encourage them to take care to avoid running into other children, and to dodge and swerve to escape the bear's clutches. The first child caught becomes the bear in the next game.

Support and extension
Have an adult play the grumpy old bear with younger children until they are familiar with the game. With older children, the bear can choose actions for the children to carry out as they run away, such as, 'You're my hopping children!'

Further ideas
■ Lie a blanket on the floor and place a teddy bear in the centre. The children pick up the blanket by the edges and, working together, toss the bear up and down. See how high the bear can fly.
■ Use a teddy bear to play 'Teddy says' instead of 'Simon says'.
■ Challenge pairs of children to carry a bear from one end of the room to the other without using their hands.

Sheep pen

What you need
Just the children.

What to do
The aim of the game is for the farmer to round up the sheep into the pen. Choose five children to act as the sheep. Have the rest of the group hold hands and form a circle to make the sheep pen. An adult can play the farmer.

When the farmer says, 'Open the pen', the children in the circle hold their hands up high. When the farmer says, 'Run, sheep, run', the five sheep run in and out, across and through the raised arms of the children forming the pen. The sheep may like to accompany the game with 'baa' noises.

When the farmer says, 'Close the pen', the children lower their arms. Any of the sheep caught inside the circle have been penned and sit in the centre of the circle. Continue the game until all the sheep have been penned.

Ensure that the children move freely, yet safely, between and under the arms of the children forming the pen, respecting their space and negotiating the area around them. Repeat the game choosing different children as the sheep.

Support and extension
Emphasise the idea of 'inside' and 'outside' with younger children. Play the game with more than five sheep with older children.

Further ideas
■ Make a lamb mask by covering a paper plate with cotton-wool balls around the outside. Draw a lamb's face in the centre. Cut out ears, cover in cotton wool and staple to the top of the plate. Attach a stick to the back of the plate for the children to hold.
■ Count sheep when trying to sleep by having three children sit under a blanket as if they are in bed. The rest of the group skips past them like sheep, one at a time, while the children under the blanket count out loud. As the last sheep goes past, the three children pretend to fall asleep.
■ Sing 'Baa Baa Black Sheep'. Find three large paper bags and number them. Ask the children to find three things in the room to count into the bags, until they are full, as in the nursery rhyme.

LEARNING OBJECTIVES
STEPPING STONE
Move freely with pleasure and confidence.

EARLY LEARNING GOAL
Move with confidence, imagination and in safety. (PD)

GROUP SIZE
15 or more children.

HOME LINKS
Invite agile parents and carers to take part in the 'Sheep pen' game.

Lily pads

What you need
Four hoops; maracas.

What to do
Spread out four hoops on the floor and explain to the children that these are lily pads floating on a pond. Ask the children to squat on their haunches with their hands on the floor and jump like a frog around the room.

Have an adult pretend to be a snake and arrive hissing and shaking maracas (or a home-made shaker of rice or dried peas in a sealed yoghurt pot). The snake is looking for lunch and the children must hop to safety on a lily pad as quickly as possible.

However, only three frogs are allowed on any one lily pad. Before they can jump into the hoop they have to count how many frogs are already there and decide if there is room for them.

Encourage the children to use language such as, 'too many' or, 'one more'. If a hoop is full they must hop to another one before being caught by the snake. If they are caught they sit out until the next game. See who is the last frog left in the game.

Support and extension
Have an adult help younger children with counting the number of frogs on the lily pads. Allow older children to take turns as the snake and change the number of frogs allowed on the lily pads each round of the game, depending upon the number of children playing.

Further ideas
■ Read frog stories, such as 'The Frog Prince' (Traditional), and sing songs, including 'Five Little Speckled Frogs'.
■ Look at the life cycle of a frog, from frogspawn to tadpole to frog. Make frogspawn using bubble wrap with a black dot in the centre. Cut tadpoles out of black shiny paper and make frogs from clay or Plasticine.
■ Use musical instruments, such as sandblocks or guiros, to make frog noises or try running a wooden spoon along the ridges of an empty plastic bottle.

Jet pilot

What you need
Chalk (or tape).

What to do
Chalk two long lines on the ground at either end of the playing area to represent airports. If playing the game indoors, use tape on the floor. Choose one child to act as the captain.

Divide the rest of the children into two groups. One group stands behind one of the lines and the other group stands behind the other line. When the captain says, 'Take off!', all the pilots run with their arms outstretched to represent the wings of a plane and making jet noises, to the opposite airport.

Ensure that the children are aware of other children running towards them and that they negotiate their flight path without bumping into anyone.

If the captain calls, 'Dive!', all the children run crouching low on the ground for a while and if the captain calls, 'Loop the loop!', everyone runs around in a small circle before continuing to the airport. When everyone has reached their destination, repeat the game with a different captain.

Support and extension
With younger children, play the game with small groups to avoid collisions. Challenge older children to have one group hold hands as they run while the other group runs underneath their arms.

Further ideas
■ Create an airport in the role-play area. Use chairs to make an aeroplane and provide headsets for the captain and the co-pilot using headphones from the listening centre. Use small suitcases and bags for luggage for the passengers. Around the walls display pictures and photographs of holiday destinations from brochures. Make an airport check-in desk with a telephone and provide boarding tickets for the check-in clerk to issue to passengers before they board the plane. Have trays for stewards to serve snacks.

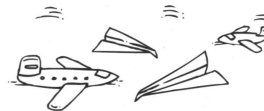

■ Collect pictures of cars, boats and aeroplanes. Prepare large sheets of paper to represent air, land and sea, and ask the children to take turns choosing a picture and placing it on the correct background.

Magog the dragon

What you need
Just the children.

What to do
Let the children help Magog the dragon grow as he walks around a village looking for his dinner. Choose a child to be Magog. The rest of the group pretend to be the children in a village and stand in a large circle with their hands on their heads to represent the roof of the house they are hiding in.

Encourage the child playing Magog to think how a dragon might move and create a dragon walk. The dragon walks around the inside of the circle, searching the village for food, saying:

> *I'm Magog the dragon,*
> *I'm big and fierce too.*
> *I want my dinner –*
> *And I want to eat YOU!*

As the dragon says, 'YOU!', it suddenly stops by one of the children in the circle and points a finger at them. That child then leaves the circle and holds the waist of the dragon, becoming a part of him as he is 'eaten'. Encourage the children to work together when moving behind the dragon, keeping contact and being ready to stop and start whenever the dragon does. Have the children join in with the dragon's rhyme as they are chosen.

The dragon continues around the village while all the children await their turn to join in. The last child left in the village becomes the next dragon and the game begins again.

Support and extension
Have helpers nearby to provide support and assistance for younger children. Older children can take the lead for young children and help to reinforce the actions of the game.

Further idea
■ Cut two dragon shapes out of green paper for each child and draw on faces and wings. Punch holes around the edges of the shapes using a hole-punch and let the children lace them together with yarn.

Over the mountain

What you need
Just the children.

What to do
Let the children explore different ways of crossing the mountain. Ask them to hold hands and stand side by side in a long line, at one end of the playing area. Have an adult call out the type of steps for the children to take, and how many. Suggested movements could be:

Three giant steps (in a loud voice)
Four baby steps (in a tiny voice)
Five kangaroo jumps
Two penguin steps (shuffle on knees)
Six boogie steps
Three duck steps (waddle).

When the chidlren are familiar with all the movements, have them advance together towards the other side of the playing area, carrying out the appropriate steps as they are called out. As they do so, encourage the children to join in with the following rhyme to the tune of 'Here We Go Round the Mulberry Bush':

This is the way we cross the mountain,
Cross the mountain, cross the mountain.
This is the way we cross the mountain,
On a cold and frosty morning.

If the leader shouts, 'Avalanche!' all the children turn around and run as fast as they can back to the start, join hands and begin again.

Support and extension
Keep group sizes small with younger children and use more simple steps to move forward to. Encourage older children to think of ways of moving that begin with a specific letter, such as 's' for skate, swim, skip or squirm, and let them take turns to call out the steps.

Further ideas
■ Ask the children to imagine they are walking along carrying a heavy suitcase (one hand), balancing a cup and saucer of hot tea or carrying a big, heavy box (two hands), or holding something very fragile. Let them pretend to pass the object to another child.
■ Have snail races where the children wriggle along on their backs.
■ Provide a selection of old shoes of all sizes (men's, ladies', older children's and babies'). Let the children experiment with walking in the shoes, taking large steps in the men's shoes, small steps when trying to fit their feet into shoes too small and so on.

Clothes dash

LEARNING OBJECTIVES
STEPPING STONE
Show increasing control over clothing and fastenings.

EARLY LEARNING GOAL
Move with control and coordination. (PD)

GROUP SIZE
12 children.

What you need
12 assorted items of clothes.

What to do
Encourage the children to play a game that involves dressing themselves in clothes and becoming familiar with an assortment of different types of fastenings. Divide the children into two teams and have them stand in a line, one behind the other, at one end of the room.

At the other end of the room, place an assortment of clothes, enough for one item of clothing for each child, in front of each team. Include clothes with a variety of fastenings, such as zips, buttons, Velcro, poppers and toggles, and also include gloves and shoes with buckles or Velcro fastenings.

On a signal, the first child from each team runs to the clothes, takes an item and puts it on, making sure all the fastenings are done up before running back to their team. The next child then runs to the clothes and so on.

See which team can have all its members dressed in the clothes the quickest. Play the game again, this time asking the children to remove the item of clothing they are wearing.

Support and extension
Keep clothes simple and provide a helper for each team to assist younger children when dressing if necessary. Challenge older children with more difficult fastenings and laces on shows for those who are learning to tie shoelaces.

Further ideas
■ Choose six children to stand in a line in front of the rest of the group. While all the children close their eyes, have one of the six hide (a table turned on its side nearby provides a good hiding place) while the rest of the children decide which child is missing and what clothes they were wearing.

■ Dress a doll in as many clothes as possible. At circle time, pass the doll around while music is played. When the music stops, the child holding the doll takes an article of clothing off. When the doll is undressed place the clothes in the centre of the circle and play the game again, this time replacing an item of clothing when the music stops.

HOME LINKS
Encourage parents and carers to allow their child plenty of time to dress themselves in the morning and undress themselves at night.

Action rhymes and songs

The repetition of words and actions in these rhymes and songs will help develop and reinforce the skills the children are learning. Encourage the children to use their imagination and to express themselves freely when acting out different roles.

Body parts

What you need
The photocopiable sheet 'I have one head' on page 76.

What to do
Begin by asking the children to count how many various body parts they have. How many heads? Can they nod and shake their head? Can they make any other movements using their head?

Ask the children how many noses they have. See if they can wiggle their nose. Challenge the children to touch their nose with different parts of their body, such as a knee, foot or finger. Ask them to tell you how many eyes they have. Encourage them to blink both their eyes and then see if they can wink one eye. See if the children can think of other actions they can do with their eyes, such as roll or cross them.

Next, ask them to tell you how many hands they have. Ask them if they can wave one hand. Can the children suggest actions to do with two hands, such as clapping or praying? Let the children tell you the number of feet they have. Challenge them to find ways to use one foot, such as hop or balance. Then, have them think of ways of using two feet, jumping or skipping, for example.

Now, ask the children to count how many fingers they have on one hand and then on two hands. Discuss the many things that they can do with their fingers, such as tickling, wriggling, playing the piano, fastening buttons and so on. Encourage all the children in the group to take part in the action rhyme 'I have one head'.

Support and extension
Give younger children plenty of opportunity to explore the ways that their bodies are capable of moving before participating in the action rhyme. Encourage older children to think of more body parts to move and incorporate them into the rhyme.

Further ideas
■ Give children the opportunity to finger-paint while listening to music.
■ Challenge the children to paint a picture without using their hands, or using their less-dominant hand.

LEARNING OBJECTIVES
STEPPING STONE
Move body position as necessary.

EARLY LEARNING GOAL
Show awareness of space, of themselves and of others. (PD)

GROUP SIZE
Any size.

HOME LINKS
Send home a copy of the photocopiable sheet 'I have one head' with each child to perform with members of their family.

Moon walk

What you need
Tape recorder or CD player; suitable music.

What to do
Ask the children to imagine what they think it might be like to walk on the moon. Practise walking with slow, floating movements and play suitable music, such as 'Ride of the Valkyries' by Wagner or anything by Jean-Michel Jarre, for the children to create their 'moon-walk dance' to.

Have the children hold hands in a circle in order to act out a space journey. Begin by asking the children to crouch, count down from ten to one and then blast off by jumping up. Then, they should start to move around the circle, getting faster and faster.

Ask the children to slow down and stop as they land on the moon and then pretend to open the hatch of the spaceship, climb down the ladder and walk on the moon.

Choose a child as the first astronaut and say the following action rhyme. At the end of each verse, encourage another child to join hands with the astronaut before them and float around together.

One little astronaut, floating out in space,
A great big smile upon his face.
He had such fun walking on the moon
He called another astronaut to join him soon.

Two little astronauts, (and so on)

Continue until all ten children are holding hands in a line. Finish the last verse with the line: 'But now it was time to go back home.' Have the children climb back into their spaceship and do everything in reverse until they land back on Earth.

Support and extension
Have a helper play alongside younger children to help develop the activity. Older children can play the game with increasing numbers of astronauts.

Further idea
■ Create a moonscape in the role-play area. Scatter cushions around the floor and cover them with white sheets. Make moon boots by attaching large pieces of sponge to children's shoes using rubber bands. Tape old plastic bottles and hoses together to make breathing apparatus. Make a space helmet out of a cardboard box painted silver. Cut a circle out of the front and replace with cling film.

The marmalade cat

What you need
Just the children.

What to do
Ask the children to explore how cats and mice move by washing, yawning and stretching like cats, and creeping on tiptoe like mice.

Choose a child as the marmalade cat while the rest of the group are mice. Ask the children to join in with the following action rhyme:

The marmalade cat is sleeping,
Sleeping quietly in the house.
(cat curls up and pretends to be asleep)

The little mice are creeping,
Creeping silently through the house.
(mice creep on tiptoe around the cat)

The marmalade cat is waking,
Waking slowly in the house.
(cat sits up, stretches and yawns)

The little mice are frightened,
Very frightened in the house.
(mice run around the cat looking scared)

The marmalade cat is chasing,
Chasing quickly in the house.
(cat chases the mice and tries to catch them)

The little mice are squeaking,
Squeaking loudly in the house.
(mice run away squeaking and the first mouse
caught becomes the next cat)

Support and extension
Have an adult take the part of the cat to lead younger children in the action rhyme. Encourage older children to put as much detail as possible into their cat and mouse movements.

Further ideas
■ Say the nursery rhyme 'The Three Little Kittens' with the children. Draw three kittens on paper and cut them out. Cut out three pairs of mittens and colour each pair a different colour. Mix up the mittens and ask the children to take turns to match a pair for each kitten.
■ Play a circle game called 'Cats and mice'. Go around the circle naming the children alternately 'cat' or 'mouse'. When you call out the letter 'c', all the children who are cats jump up and run around the circle miaowing. When you call 'm' for mouse, all the mice jump up and run around squeaking.

LEARNING OBJECTIVES
STEPPING STONE
Play alongside other children who are engaged in the same theme.

EARLY LEARNING GOAL
Use their imagination in art and design, music, dance, imaginative and role play and stories. (CD)

GROUP SIZE
Five or more children.

HOME LINKS
Invite a willing parent or carer who has a cat or a mouse as a pet to bring it in to show to the group. Talk about the correct way to look after them and watch carefully how they move.

Happy families

What you need
The photocopiable sheet 'Here comes daddy' on page 77.

What to do
Talk about the various people who make up a family group and ensure that you discuss all types of families. It is helpful if you familiarise yourself with the children's parents, siblings, grandparents and so on for this activity.

Let each child take turns to discuss the members of their family. Draw the children's attention to the growth process, how newly born babies in their family grow into toddlers, children, teenagers, adults and then elderly grandparents or great-grandparents.

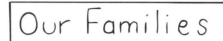

Ask the children to think about how the different family members might walk down the street. Introduce suitable vocabulary, such as 'stride', 'tramp', 'march', 'skip', 'shuffle', 'stroll', 'creep' or 'prance'. For example, an old person could shuffle in a tired way, children could run and skip, a baby could toddle or crawl and men could stride or march. Then, encourage the children to join in with the action rhyme, 'Here comes daddy'.

Support and extension
Let younger children take part in one verse of the action rhyme per session, building up to the complete rhyme in stages. Provide dressing-up clothes and props for older children to choose when participating in the rhyme and encourage them to suggest other family members and how they could move.

Further ideas
■ Make portraits of family members using paper plates. Provide yarn, cotton wool, straw, scraps of paper, fabric and felt-tipped pens to create the portraits and exhibit them on an 'Our families' display.
■ Make a graph showing the members of each child's family.
■ Play an 'Action' game by designating each corner of the room to four family members, for example, mummy, daddy, grandma and baby. Have the children dance around the room to music and when the music stops call out a family member. The children must move to that corner using the appropriate action.

LEARNING OBJECTIVES

STEPPING STONE
Talk freely about their home and community.

EARLY LEARNING GOAL
Respond to significant experiences, showing a range of feelings when appropriate. (PSED)

GROUP SIZE
Ten to 15 children.

HOME LINKS
Send the rhyme home, and ask parents and carers to help their children learn it.

Ten fine soldiers

What you need
Drum.

What to do
Ask the group to pretend that they are soldiers and march around the room with knees high and a straight back, holding their head tall and swinging their arms. Have an adult beat a drum to a steady rhythm and see if the children can try and march in step to the drum.

Introduce the following number rhyme to the children and encourage them to join in. Begin by having the soldiers stand in a line, shoulder to shoulder. Choose a child to act as the sergeant and say, 'March!' where appropriate.

> *Ten fine soldiers standing in a row,*
> *The sergeant says 'march!' and off they go.*
> *They march to the left,*
> *one-two, one-two, one-two,*
> *They march to the right,*
> *one-two, one-two, one-two,*
> *Then one little soldier marched out of sight.*
>
> *Nine fine soldiers… (and so on)*

Have the soldiers begin marching around in a circle, starting with the child on the left of the line, to the beat 'one-two'. Re-form the line, then have the child on the right of the line lead the soldiers in a circle to the right.

The last soldier in the line leaves the circle and marches away to sit down during the last line of the rhyme. Continue until all the soldiers have marched out of sight.

Support and extension
Have an adult act as the sergeant and lead the soldiers, helping younger children to keep in time. Older children can take turns to beat the drum, indicating whether to march fast or slow.

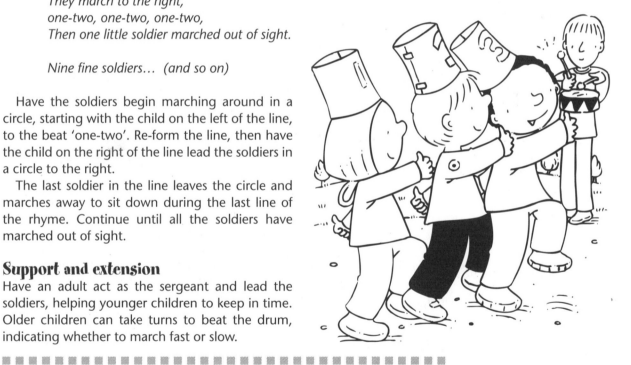

Further ideas
■ Make hats for the soldiers to wear as they take part in the action rhyme. Fold and tape card into cylinder shapes to fit the children's heads. Number the hats 1 to 10 and ask the children to get themselves into the correct order in the line before starting the rhyme.
■ Say the rhyme 'Ten Fat Sausages' and mark out a frying pan on the floor using tape, chalk or a rope. Two children 'pop' and 'bang' out of the pan at the appropriate time in each verse.

LEARNING OBJECTIVES
STEPPING STONE
Enjoy joining in with number rhymes and songs.

EARLY LEARNING GOAL
Say and use number names in order in familiar contexts. (MD)

GROUP SIZE
Ten children.

HOME LINKS
Ask parents and carers to take their child on a 'soldier walk' and see if their child can collect and count ten different things.

Alphabet actions

What you need
Just the children.

What to do
Introduce the letter 'd' to the children and practise saying the phonetic sound of 'd,d,d'. Ask them if anyone can suggest any words beginning with 'd'. Encourage the children to join in with the first verse of the action rhyme:

> *If you want to dance for me, you must say the letter 'd'.*
> *(dance around the room making the sound 'd,d,d')*

Introduce the letter 'j' in a similar way and say the rhyme:

> *If you like to jump all day, can you say the letter 'j'?*
> *(jump around the room saying 'j,j,j')*

Continue with the rest of the rhyme as follows:

> *Twirl like a top as fast as can be,*
> *If you can say the letter 't'.*

> *If a boxer you'd like to be,*
> *Punch, punch, punch the letter 'p'.*

> *A game of football we can play,*
> *If you kick the letter 'k'.*

> *Zigzag, zigzag, like I said,*
> *Back and fore like the letter 'z'.*

> *Like a caterpillar in a tree,*
> *Crawl, crawl, crawl if you say 'c'.*

> *Stamp and stamp and stamp, oh yes,*
> *Stamp very hard to the letter 's'.*

Support and extension
Introduce the rhyme one letter per session for younger children and have a helper nearby to help with the sounds and actions. Challenge older children to see if they can suggest any other letters together with an appropriate action, such as hopping to 'h' or bending to 'b'.

Further ideas
■ Let each child fill in a copy of the photocopiable sheet 'I can ...' located on page 78.
■ Cut out large circles of white paper and write large black letters on them. Place them on the floor and see if the children can stamp around the circle marked 's' and so on.
■ Make large letters on the ground using rope or chalk and walk, tiptoe or hop along them while making the letter sound.

The world keeps spinning

What you need
Just the children.

What to do
Take the children on a local walk and encourage them to listen to, and look closely at the things around them, both natural and man-made.

Explain in simple words that the earth spins around the sun and that it takes one whole year to do so. You can demonstrate this by using one large ball and one small ball.

Introduce the following action rhyme:

> *The sun comes up at the start of the day,*
> *(on tiptoe, make large circle over head)*
> *Down comes the rain when the skies are grey,*
> *(wriggle fingers down to the floor)*
> *The sun comes up, the rain falls down,*
> *(show the sun and the rain again)*
> *And the world keeps spinning as it turns around.*
> *(twirl around, arms outstretched)*

> *The waves roll in on the golden sand,*
> *(roly-poly hands inwards towards body)*
> *Out sail the boats far away from land,*
> *(roly-poly hands outwards away from body)*
> *The waves roll in, the boats sail out,*
> *(show the waves and the boats again)*
> *And the world keeps spinning as it turns around.*
> *(twirl around, arms outstretched)*

> *Under the ground the worms wriggle by,*
> *(wriggle on tummy)*
> *Over the treetops the birds fly high,*
> *(flap arms)*
> *Worms wriggle by, birds fly high,*
> *(show worms and birds again)*
> *And the world keeps spinning as it turns around.*
> *(twirl around, arms outstretched)*

Support and extension
Keep the concept simple for younger children; lie quietly on a blanket outdoors and look and listen carefully. Emphasise the spatial language with older children.

Further idea
■ Enjoy the outdoors as much as possible. Eat snacks outside, read stories, play music to dance to and hang dressing-up clothes from a fence or tree for the children to use.

Mean machines

What you need
Just the children.

What to do
Talk about the various types of machines the children may find in different rooms of their house. Remind them that machines make things easier for us.

Ask the children to try and describe the noises the machines make, such as rattle, roar, click, tick or whirr. Encourage them to think of movements made by machines, for example, pump, chop and spin around and around.

Encourage the group to join in with the action rhyme 'Mean machines' as follows:

> *Spinning wheels and clocks that tick,*
> *(make circling motions with hands and arms)*
> *Computers printing, click, clack, click,*
> *(pretend to type with fingers)*
> *Bicycle chains rattling round and round,*
> *(move hands in circular motions)*
> *Engines pumping up and down,*
> *(pump legs up and down, raising knees high)*
> *Motors running fast and slow,*
> *(run on the spot, fast and slow)*
> *Pushing handles to and fro,*
> *(pretend to push handles with both hands)*
> *Clanking, clonking clockwork toys,*
> *(walk stiffly like clockwork toy)*
> *Why do machines make so much noise?*
> *(cover hands with ears)*
> *Whirr, clang, hum and POP,*
> *(clap hands on POP)*
> *I wish that I could make them STOP!*
> *(raise hands in 'stop' gesture)*

Repeat the rhyme until the children are familiar with it and can repeat the actions confidently.

Support and extension
Allow younger children to sit and watch until they feel confident to join in with this rhyme. With older children, repeat the rhyme, beginning slowly and making the machine work faster and faster, until they suddenly stop.

Further ideas
■ Collect cogs, screws, bolts and so on and press them into small squares of clay or play dough.
■ Make machine music by using metal objects, such as tapping cutlery together or jangling metal objects in a box.

Dancing feet

What you need
Tape recorder or CD player; variety of music.

What to do
Gather a variety of musical tapes or CDs. Include as many different types of music as possible, such as rap, reggae, disco, choral, nursery rhymes, classical, orchestral, folk, rock, world music and the latest favourite chart song.

Encourage the children to listen carefully to the music and think how it makes them feel as they dance to the various rhythms and beats. See if the dancers can join in with the following action rhyme, matching their dance to the words of the rhyme:

> *Can you see my dancing feet,*
> *Dancing to the happy beat?*
> *Sometimes fast and sometimes slow,*
> *Sometimes high and sometimes low.*
> *They twirl and tap and shake and prance,*
> *They boogie, twist and jig a dance.*
>
> *Can you see my dancing feet,*
> *Dancing to the noisy beat?*
> *Sometimes heavy and sometimes strong,*
> *Sometimes loud and sometimes long.*
> *They jump and leap and march and bound,*
> *They kick and stamp upon the ground.*
>
> *Can you see my dancing feet,*
> *Dancing to the gentle beat?*
> *Come along and dance with me,*
> *Dance just like the feet you see.*
> *We'll tiptoe, bounce and skip and hop,*
> *Then we'll spin and spin and stop.*

Support and extension
Allow younger children time to experiment freely with their dancing before joining in with the rhyme. Encourage older children to dance first to give ideas and inspire confidence in the younger ones.

Further ideas
■ Glue pennies (using strong glue) to the toe and heel of old shoes to use for tap dancing.
■ Ask the children to bring in their favourite music from home and create a radio station. Name the station and play the music during the day. Make a microphone out of a cardboard tube and make announcements through the radio for snack time, playtime, lunchtime and so on.
■ Cut out shoe shapes and place them on the floor to make a pattern for the children to follow.

Jack-in-the-box

What you need
Just the children.

What to do
Explain to the children that they are going to pretend to be a Jack-in-the-box in a toyshop. Ask them to sit in a row as if on a shelf. Encourage the children to join in with the following action rhyme:

> *I'm a Jack-in-the-box*
> *On a shelf in a shop,*
> *(crouch down, hands over head to form lid of box)*
> *Who will come and buy me?*
> *I jump up high when you open my lid.*
> *Are you ready, one, two, three!*
> *(jump up on 'three' and waggle head, body and arms)*

Choose a child to take the part of a customer who comes into the shop and wants to buy a Jack-in-the-box. Have this child approach one of the 'toys' and say the following rhyme:

> *I want a toy – a Jack-in-the-box,*
> *(walks along looking at all the toys)*
> *Which one shall I try?*
> *(stops in front of one and points)*
> *Pop up, go down, pop up, go down*
> *(that Jack-in-the-box jumps up and down)*
> *Which one shall I buy?*

Ask the customer to choose a selection of Jack-in-the-boxes to perform for them and then select the one they think is the best and take it from the shop. The chosen Jack-in-the-box becomes the next customer.

Support and extension
With younger children, have an adult play the part of the customer to help guide the activity. Vary the order and speed of the Jack-in-the-box actions in the third line for older children to try and follow.

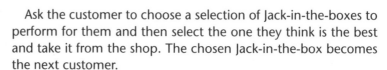

Further ideas
■ Vary the rhyme by asking the children to think of other toys, such as a spinning top, train or puppet, and decide on the movements to make.
■ Make a simple stick puppet of 'Jack'. The children can make him pop up behind tables, cupboards or books.
■ Make a box using blankets or building blocks for the children to hide in as Jack and then pop out of.

Traditional stories and rhymes

Children enjoy familiar stories and rhymes and often ask for them to be repeated. In this chapter movement and dance is incorporated to give children opportunities to join in with the retelling of traditional tales and nursery rhymes.

Incy Wincy Spider

What you need
Just the children.

What to do
Sing the rhyme 'Incy Wincy Spider' and encourage the children to join in. Ask them to imagine how they think a spider might move and then create a 'spider dance'. Introduce words, such as 'creeping', 'scuttling' and 'scurrying', and discuss how a spider will move very quickly and then stop suddenly and stay very still.

Choose six children to pretend to be spiders. The rest of the group form a circle of 'raindrops'. Have the spiders stand in the middle of the circle.

Recite the rhyme 'Incy Wincy Spider' together. When the line, 'Washed the spider out' is reached, all the children who are spiders scuttle away as fast as they can while the raindrops try to catch them.

When all the spiders have been caught, have them return to the centre of the circle and then continue with the rest of the rhyme. The first six children to catch the spiders can become the spiders in the next game.

Support and extension
Very young children enjoy this rhyme; encourage them to listen and join in before taking part in the activity. Ask older children to form spiderwebs by getting into groups of four. See if they can trap a spider in the middle of their web. Who can trap the most spiders?

Further ideas
■ Make headbands for the spiders to wear when enjoying the activity. Cut a strip of black paper (about 5cm wide) to fit the child's head. Accordion fold eight more strips of paper for the spider's legs and staple them to the headband. Staple a black circle to the front and draw on a spider's face.
■ Make a web by doing a black marble painting on white paper and place a spider in the web.
■ Go on a walk and collect spiders in a large jar. Place earth in the bottom and add a few twigs and leaves. Observe the spiders for a day or two and then release them.

LEARNING OBJECTIVES
STEPPING STONE
Listen to favourite nursery rhymes, stories and songs. Join in with repeated refrains, anticipating key events and important phrases.

EARLY LEARNING GOAL
Listen with enjoyment, and respond to stories, songs and other music, rhymes and poems and make up their own stories, songs, rhymes and poems. (CLL)

GROUP SIZE
20 or more children.

HOME LINKS
Send a letter home to parents and carers with ideas for making spiders to accompany the rhyme 'Incy Wincy Spider'.

Cinderella's duster

What you need
Just the children.

What to do
Briefly remind the children of the story of 'Cinderella' (Traditional) and explain that you are going to act out the story through dance. Give each child in the group an imaginary duster. Tell them that they must clean the house with the duster as ordered by the ugly sisters.

Encourage them to explore the space around them by stretching up high to dust the ceilings, bending down low to clean the floors, dusting the walls with zigzag movements and cleaning the windows with circular motions. Halfway through the activity call, 'Pumpkin!' and explain that this is a signal for the children to change the duster into their other hand.

Continue with the story by asking the children to move on tiptoe like the Good Fairy, waving a magic wand. Then, ask them to creep like mice before they become the horses and prance around pulling the coach. Next, ask the children to find a partner and dance at the ball with the Prince.

Finally, have the children pretend to search everywhere for the lost slipper. Tell the children that if you call out, 'Ugly Sisters!' at any time, they must immediately stop and drop to the floor, before continuing with their dance.

Support and extension
Have an adult near younger children to help with suggestions for their dances. Encourage older children to retell the story in their own words and build up a more complex sequence of actions.

Further idea
■ Play 'Hunt the slipper' by having the children sit in a circle. Provide a fancy shoe and give it to a child in the circle who holds it behind their back. Choose a child to sit in the centre of the circle with their eyes closed. Play music and have the children pass the slipper around the circle behind their backs. When the music stops, the child in the middle opens their eyes and has three guesses as to who has the slipper. If they are correct they change places.

Snow White

What you need
Just the children.

What to do
Briefly recall the events in the story of 'Snow White and the Seven Dwarfs' (Traditional) with the children. Pay particular attention to the rhyme spoken into the mirror by Snow White's wicked stepmother: 'Mirror, mirror, on the wall, who is the fairest one of all?'

Explain that the children are going to play a 'Copying' game. Ask everyone to find a partner, to stand facing them and to decide who will lead and who will copy. Ask the children to join in with the following rhyme:

> Mirror, mirror, on the wall,
> I wonder who you can see.
> When I raise my arm like this
> You look a lot like me.

Try and introduce vocabulary, such as 'follow', 'repeat', 'first', 'next', 'after', 'beside' and 'facing', when explaining to the children that if the first child raises their arm, their partner 'repeats' the action or 'follows' them in their movements.

Encourage the children to suggest other movements they could use in the rhyme, such as, 'When I shake my head like this'. As well as moving face to face, see if the children can move side by side when skipping, hopping, jumping or galloping.

Support and extension
Keep movements simple for younger children. Invite older children to act as a partner for a younger child and provide movements for them to mirror.

Further ideas
■ Make mirrors for each child by covering a piece of card (10 x 15cm) with aluminium foil. Add a frame to the front.
■ Ask the children to think of as many words as they can to describe a mirror, such as 'shiny', 'bright' and silvery. Write them down on pieces of shiny paper and stick them to a mirror.
■ Sing the following song, carrying out the actions as described and think of more of your own:

> Hi Ho, Hi Ho, it's off to school we'll go.
> We'll clean our teeth and brush our hair,
> Hi Ho, Hi Ho.

LEARNING OBJECTIVES
STEPPING STONE
Use vocabulary and forms of speech that are increasingly influenced by experience of books.

EARLY LEARNING GOAL
Extend their vocabulary, exploring the meanings and sounds of new words. (CLL)

GROUP SIZE
Six to 20 children.

HOME LINKS
Ask parents and carers to help their child choose something from home that they can see their face in and bring it to show the rest of the group.

Gingerbread men

What you need
Two skipping ropes.

What to do
First, make sure that the children are familiar with the story of 'The Gingerbread Man' (Traditional). Place the two ropes on the floor (approximately 50cm apart) to form a river.

Choose five children to take the role of gingerbread men and ask them to stand on one side of the river. The other five children should each play one of the animals in the rhyme. Ask 'the animals' to stand on the opposite side of the river.

Let the 'gingerbread men' have fun running as they say the rhyme and then jump over the river. The 'dog' captures one of the gingerbread men who then sits out of that game. Continue with the rhyme, with the appropriate animal catching one of the gingerbread men each time until there are none left.

Five little gingerbread men running through the door.
A dog ate one and that left four.

Four little gingerbread men running past a tree.
A sheep ate one and that left three.

Three little gingerbread men running straight and true.
A cow ate one and that left two.

Two little gingerbread men running just for fun.
A horse ate one and that left one.

One little gingerbread man running in the sun.
A fox ate him and that left none.

Support and extension
Help less confident children to jump across the river and take part in the chasing game to avoid being caught and 'eaten'. Increase the distance between the ropes after each verse so that older children have further to jump across the river every time.

Further ideas
■ Cut five (or ten) small gingerbread-men shapes from paper and let the children use them to practise counting.
■ Draw characters from the story on card and cut them out. Glue a small square of Velcro to the back. Glue small squares of Velcro to an old oven glove and attach the characters to the glove as you tell the story.
■ Cut out gingerbread-men shapes from brown paper and decorate with coffee grounds or tea leaves.

Twinkle, twinkle, little star

What you need
Just the children.

What to do
Sing the traditional nursery rhyme 'Twinkle, Twinkle, Little Star' with the children. Ask the group to imagine that they are a star twinkling in the sky. Let the children create a 'star dance' using quick, sparky movements, such as throwing their arms up and stretching their fingers out wide. Encourage the children to think of different ways to represent a shooting star, diving down to the floor or shooting sideways.

Create a scene where you suggest actions for the children to respond to. Begin by asking the children to lie down and pretend to be in bed asleep one night. Then, tell them that they have decided they want to go outside and look at the stars.

Quietly, have them get out of bed and dress themselves in imaginary slippers and dressing gowns. Next, ask the children to creep outside on tiptoe and look up at the stars twinkling all around them.

Sing 'Twinkle, Twinkle, Little Star' while the children perform their dance. Then explain that it is time to creep back inside, take off their slippers and dressing gowns, climb quietly back into bed and go to sleep.

Support and extension
Younger children will already know and enjoy this rhyme. Lead them slowly with clear, simple instructions as you introduce each idea. Older children can suggest their own night-time adventure and actions in response to the rhyme, adding variations such as cleaning teeth or opening and closing doors.

Further ideas
■ Cut out ten stars from paper and number them 1 to 10 using fluorescent paint. Paint the inside of a cardboard box with black paint and tape the stars inside. Let the children shine a torch into the box and identify the numbers while singing 'Twinkle, Twinkle, Little Star'.
■ Cut out star shapes with five points from card and, using crayons, give each point a different colour. Give the children five clothes pegs in the same colours to clip to the matching colour on the star.
■ Sing lullabies with the children.

Three blind mice

What you need
Tambourine.

What to do
Introduce the nursery rhyme 'Three Blind Mice' to the children and encourage
them to join in. Ensure that the children can sing the rhyme from memory.

Ask the children to pretend to be mice and creep quietly around the room
on tiptoe. Play a tambourine to accompany the mice actions. Play it fast or
slow and then stop suddenly, and encourage the children to match their
mouse movements to the music.

Then, ask all the 'mice' to form a circle. Choose a child to play the farmer's
wife who stands in the middle. Encourage everyone to join in with singing
'Three Blind Mice'. Ask them to dance their 'mice dance' around the circle.

Tell the children that on the last words, all the mice should scuttle away
to the sound of the tambourine while the farmer's wife tries to catch one of
them. The first mouse to be caught becomes the next farmer's wife.

Support and extension
Support younger children while they listen to the rhyme and then encourage
them to join in with it before participating in the game. Let older children try
closing their eyes when running away, like the blind mice in the rhyme, using
their hands to avoid bumping into others.

Further ideas
■ Place skipping ropes or a
washing-line on the ground
in various designs. Let the
children remove their shoes
and socks and follow along the
rope with their bare feet like
mice. See if they can close their
eyes and feel the way using
only their feet.
■ Cut out three mice shapes
from card. Glue three different
lengths of string to the mice as
tails. Have the children place
the mice in order according
to the length of their tail,
shortest to longest or longest
to shortest.
■ Sing 'Three Blind Mice' using
a mouse's squeak instead of the
words. Let the children suggest
other nursery rhymes that they
can squeak to.

Billy goats gruff

What you need
Two skipping ropes.

What to do
Briefly discuss the story 'The Three Billy Goats Gruff' (Traditional) with the children. Explain that they are going to play a game based on the story. Make a bridge by placing two skipping ropes side by side on the ground. Place the ropes approximately three metres apart.

Choose one child to take the role of the troll. This child stands at one end of the bridge. Explain that the rest of the group are going to be goats who want to go across. Have them line up facing the bridge and altogether they ask the troll: 'Mr Troll, Mr Troll, may we cross your bridge?'

The troll replies with a frightening roar: 'You may hop across my bridge if you are wearing the colour blue.'

All those children wearing the colour blue hop between the two ropes to the field on the other side, saying: 'Trip trap, trip trap'.

The troll then chooses a different action and a different colour until all the children have crossed the bridge.

Support and extension
Have a helper nearby to give confidence to any less secure children who may be frightened of the troll. Allow them to take turns as the troll, but whisper suggestions in their ear if necessary. Encourage older children to be specific, aiming instructions at one particular child when allowing passage over the bridge, for example: 'If you are wearing a blue striped jumper and black shorts'. Actions can be more difficult, such as hopping backwards.

■■■■■■■■■■■■■■■■■■■

Further ideas
■ As a variation, use a bench or wooden planks for the bridge and provide different shoes for the children to wear. They can tip-tap in hard shoes, flip-flop in sandals, clomp-clump in big boots or swish-swash in slippers.

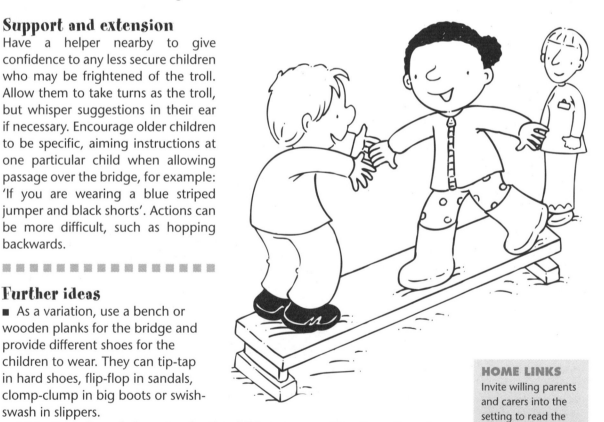

■ Make flannelboard characters for the children to use with a flannelboard when retelling the story.
■ Read the story of 'The Three Little Pigs' (Traditional) and compare the two stories (three good characters and one bad and so on).

LEARNING OBJECTIVES
STEPPING STONE
Respond to rhythm, music and story by means of gesture and movement.

EARLY LEARNING GOAL
Move with confidence, imagination and in safety. (PD)
■■■■■■■■■

GROUP SIZE
Ten to 20 children.
■■■■■■■■■

HOME LINKS
Invite willing parents and carers into the setting to read the story of 'The Three Billy Goats Gruff' to a small group of children.
■■■■■■■■■

Nursery rhyme rhythms

What you need
Ten paper plates.

What to do
Sing a selection of favourite nursery rhymes with the children. Encourage them to dance to the rhyme as they sing it, moving a different part of their body each time. For example, sing one rhyme with the children raising their elbows to each beat as they dance. Sing another rhyme with them stamping their feet, lifting their shoulders or shaking their head as they dance around.

When the children are familiar with the idea of moving to the rhythm of the rhyme, provide each child with a paper plate. Ask the children to tap the plate against a part of their body as they dance to the rhyme (on their elbow, for example). Sing another rhyme, this time asking the children to tap the plate on their knee as they dance (or their bottom or head) and so on.

Give each child a copy of the photocopiable sheet 'Sing the rhyme' on page 80. See if they can identify the rhymes shown in the pictures and sing them while tapping out the rhythm with their plate.

Support and extension
Keep to short, well-known rhymes with an easy rhythm with younger children. Older children can tap out the rhythms of longer, more complex rhymes and songs, tapping their plate on more difficult parts of the body, such as the heel or thumb.

Further ideas
■ Have the children sit in a circle. Choose a hat as the 'Nursery-rhyme hat'. Decide on a nursery rhyme for the children to recite. As the children say it, they pass the hat from one child to the next, placing it on their head. Whoever is wearing the hat when the last word is reached chooses the next rhyme.

■ Make rhythm sticks to play when singing nursery rhymes with the children. Use everyday objects which are similar to each other, such as a fork and spoon, two wooden spoons, two pencils, two empty plastic bottles or two construction pieces.

Little Red Riding Hood

What you need
Just the children.

What to do
Briefly discuss the main story points in Little Red Riding Hood (Traditional). Ask the children to identify the main characters (Little Red Riding Hood, the wolf and grandma). Choose three children to play these characters and explain that the whole group is going to play a game based on the story.

Select a site on one side of the playing area to represent Little Red Riding Hood's house. At the other end of the room have grandma's house. Ask the remainder of the children to place themselves between the two houses and stand straight and tall as if they are trees.

Have Little Red Riding Hood leave her house and make her way through the wood. As she does so, ask the trees to sing the following rhyme to the tune of 'Row, Row, Row Your Boat':

> *Here is Little Red Riding Hood,*
> *Coming through the woods.*
> *Skipping and jumping and hopping and dancing,*
> *Beware the Big Bad Wolf!*

As Little Red Riding Hood dances through the trees, ask the child representing the wolf to try and creep up and catch her before she reaches the safety of grandma's house. Tell the children representing the trees that the wolf cannot catch Little Red Riding Hood if she is touching a tree and that they can reach out to help her, but must not move.

If Little Red Riding Hood reaches grandma safely, have them join together in a dance. If not, begin the game again choosing three different children to play the characters.

Support and extension
Have an adult or older child take the part of the woodcutter and guide younger children through the trees. Let older children see who can reach grandma's house in the fastest time.

Further ideas
■ Provide props for the children to wear: a wolf mask for the wolf, a red cloak for Little Red Riding Hood and a shawl for grandma.
■ Ask children to make up their own version of the story, such as 'Little Blue Boots Boy'.

LEARNING OBJECTIVES
STEPPING STONE
Describe main story settings, events and principal characters.

EARLY LEARNING GOAL
Listen with enjoyment, and respond to stories, songs and other music, rhymes and poems and make up their own stories, songs, rhymes and poems. (CLL)

GROUP SIZE
15 to 20 children.

HOME LINKS
Ask parents and carers to discuss the danger of their child going off on their own and talking to strangers, as happened in the story.

Three little pigs

What you need
Just the children.

What to do
Talk to the group about the story of 'The Three Little Pigs' (Traditional). Explain to the children that they are going to retell the story though a dance activity. Choose six children to imagine they are the little pigs in the story with the rest of the children pretending to be wolves. Have the pigs stand in the middle of a circle pretending to build a house of straw while the wolves stand around the outside.

When the house is finished, ask the pigs to join hands and use their imagination to perform a 'happy pig dance'. Tell the children that when you call, 'The wolves are coming!', the pigs should huddle inside their pretend house while the wolves move in a circle around them saying: 'Little pigs, little pigs, let us come in!' Encourage the children to imagine how wolves would behave, prowling and growling. Have the pigs reply: 'Not by the hair on our chinny chin chin!'

Then, ask the wolves to reply: 'Then we'll huff and we'll puff and we'll blow your house in!' Ask the wolves to blow hard at the straw house while the pigs run away. The pigs should then choose another place to build their house of sticks, and the same thing happens.

Next, ask the pigs to build their house out of bricks. This time, have the wolves blow, and then run away when the house doesn't fall down. Tell the pigs that they can now celebrate by holding hands and dancing their happy pig dance again.

Support and extension
Lead younger children carefully through the story, providing useful suggestions if necessary. Encourage older children to carry out the activity as independently as possible.

Further ideas
■ Build three houses using drinking straws, twigs and LEGO. Ask the children to find out which is the strongest.
■ Make finger puppets of the characters in the story for the children to play with and re-enact the tale.
■ Look at non-fiction books about pigs.

Floppy Fiona

Fiona the rag doll was lying in a floppy heap *(pause)*. Suddenly her feet began to twitch *(pause)*, her fingers began to wiggle *(pause)* and her head began to shake *(pause)*.

Slowly Fiona struggled to sit up, but she kept flopping down again *(pause)*. She tried to lift her head, but it kept falling forward *(pause)*. Finally, she managed to hold her head up straight and look around her *(pause)*.

She saw Grizzle, the teddy bear, sitting watching her. Fiona lifted her arm to wave to him, but her arm just flopped down *(pause)*. She tried again. This time she could hold her arm in the air, but her hand dangled around loosely on the end of her wrist and then it flopped *(pause)*. She tried lifting her other arm. Ah, this was better. She was just able to wave to Grizzle before her arm sagged down *(pause)*. Grizzle smiled at her and waved back, calling her over *(pause)*.

Fiona tried to stand up, but her knees were very wobbly *(pause)*. Oops, she fell over! *(pause)*. She got up again and carefully took a step forward. Her foot waggled around on the end of her leg *(pause)*. She took another shaky step *(pause)*. Then another *(pause)*. Oh no, she collapsed again! *(pause)*. Finally, Fiona managed to stand on her two floppy legs and gradually wibbled and wobbled her way over to Grizzle *(pause)*.

Grizzle got to his feet, but this was very difficult with his stiff, furry arms and legs *(pause)*. He stomped over to meet Fiona, holding out his hands to catch her before she fell again *(pause)*. Fiona wanted to dance. She wobbled around doing her floppy, bouncy dance, dragging her partner, poor Grizzle, around on his straight little legs that wouldn't bend at all *(pause)*. Soon Grizzle had to stop and sit down *(pause)*. He was quite out of breath.

At last, when Fiona was so tired that her arms and legs and head were beginning to droop, she sagged down on the floor *(pause)*. Her head flopped forward and she collapsed in a heap and was soon fast asleep *(pause)*.

Beverley Michael

What are these hands doing?

Can you do the same?

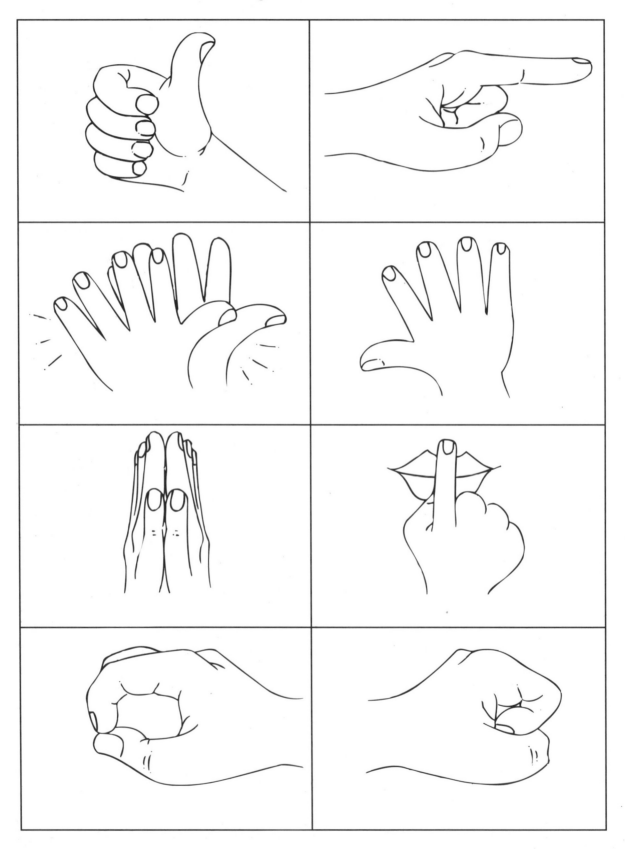

Can you fly?

Colour in the things that can fly.

The trees are growing tall

(Tune: 'The Farmer's in his Den'.)

The trees are growing tall, *(stand tall with arms stretched high)*
The trees are growing tall,
The sun shines down to help them grow, *(make a circle with arms)*
The trees are growing tall.

The trees are growing roots, *(bend down and touch floor)*
The trees are growing roots,
The rain comes down to water them, *(wriggle fingers down for rain)*
The trees are growing roots.

The trees are growing leaves, *(wave and curl arms)*
The trees are growing leaves,
Now spring is here and buds appear, *(shoot out arms, fingers stretched)*
The trees are growing leaves.

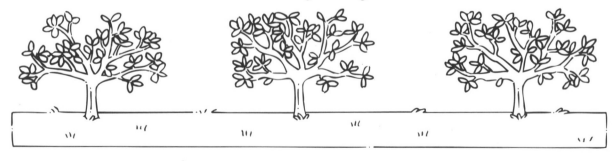

Beverley Michael

Under the big top

Under the big top what can I see?
I can see a funny clown doing tricks for me.
Under the big top what can I see?
I can see horses prancing round for me.
Under the big top what can I see?
I can see tightrope walkers, balancing for me.
Under the big top what can I see?
I can see jugglers, juggling things for me.
Under the big top what can I see?
I can see acrobats, rolling round for me.
Under the big top what can I see?
I can see a ringmaster, calling out for ME!

Beverley Michael

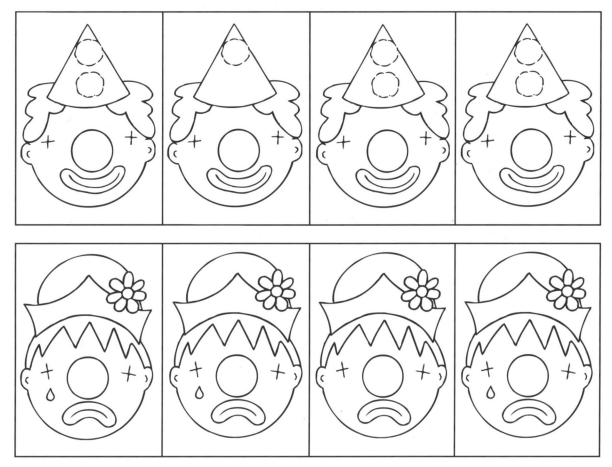

Can you draw a circle around the clown that is different?

Monster moods

Can you tell what the monsters in the pictures are feeling?

Noah and the big rain

Noah was building an enormous ship. It had to be big enough to hold Noah and his family and two of every animal in the world. It was hard work. Noah was building his ship, called an Ark, out of wood and he and his sons had to chop down the trees *(pause)*. Then saw the wood *(pause)* and hammer nails into the wood *(pause)*. Everyone thought Noah was very silly. They laughed and pointed at him *(pause)*. 'Fancy building such a great big ship!' they cried *(pause)*.

But Noah took no notice. He was building his Ark for a special reason. God had spoken to him. God was sad because all the people were doing bad things, so He was sending a big rain. God said the rain would flood the land and the only way for Noah to be safe was to build an Ark for his family and all the animals.

Soon it was time for the animals to enter the Ark. Two by two, the elephants lumbered on *(pause)*. Then the lions prowled on, roaring at everyone *(pause)*. Two by two, kangaroos and frogs hopped on to the Ark *(pause)*. Horses trotted on, tossing their heads *(pause)* and bears stalked on *(pause)*. Two by two, snakes slithered on *(pause)* and two birds of every size and colour flew on *(pause)*. Spiders and caterpillars and insects of every kind crawled on to the enormous Ark *(pause)*. They were just in time. Lightning flashed *(pause)*, thunder crashed *(pause)* and it began to rain. And it rained. And it rained. It rained for 40 days and 40 nights *(pause)*.

First of all water covered the flowers, and then the trees. Soon the water covered the tallest mountains. There was water everywhere. It swirled and poured and rushed and gushed *(pause)*. Water covered the land.

Then suddenly the big rain stopped *(pause)*. Slowly the water began to go down. The tops of the mighty mountains appeared. Then the trees showed tall and straight once more *(pause)*. Even the smallest flowers peeped out from under the water *(pause)*. When Noah opened the doors of the Ark, the animals were happy to be on land again. They ran and galloped and hopped and slithered and crawled and flew off as fast as they could *(pause)*.

Noah thanked God for keeping him, his family and all the creatures safe. God promised that he would never send another flood. Noah gazed up in wonder as the sun came out and a beautiful rainbow appeared in the sky *(pause)*.

Beverley Michael

Buzzing bees

Give each bee a partner by making sets of two.

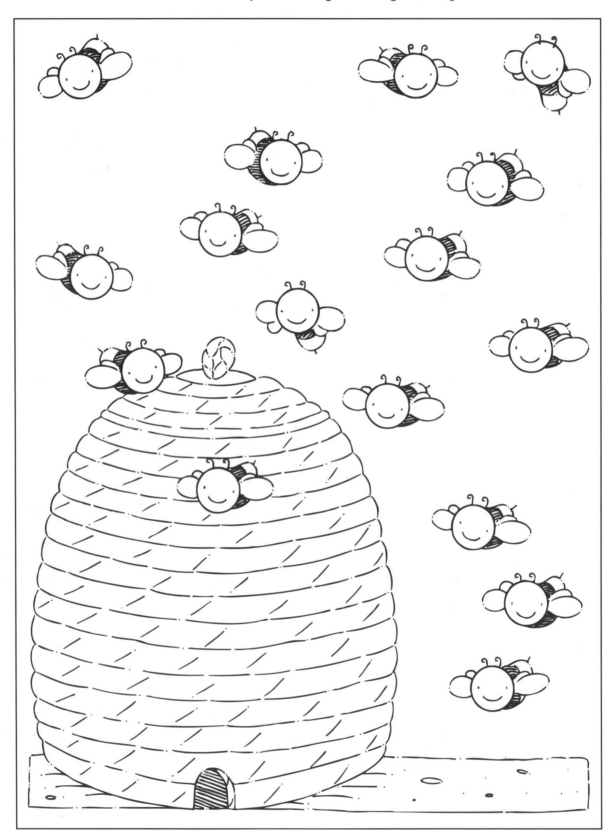

Lily pad game

Throw a dice and see who can cross the lily pads first. Use a counter as your frog.

I have one head

I have one head to nod, nod, nod,
I have one head to shake, shake, shake,
Nod, nod, nod, Shake, shake, shake,
That's what I can do, can you?

I have one nose to wiggle, wiggle, wiggle,
I have one tummy to jiggle, jiggle, jiggle,
Wiggle, wiggle, wiggle, Jiggle, jiggle, jiggle,
That's what I can do, can you?

I have one eye to wink, wink, wink,
I have two eyes to blink, blink, blink,
Wink, wink, wink, Blink, blink, blink,
That's what I can do, can you?

I have one foot to hop, hop, hop,
I have two feet to jump, jump, jump,
Hop, hop, hop, Jump, jump, jump,
That's what I can do, can you?

I have five fingers to wriggle, wriggle, wriggle,
I have ten fingers to tickle, tickle, tickle,
Wriggle, wriggle, wriggle, Tickle, tickle, tickle,
That's what I can do, can you?

One head to nod, One head to shake,
One nose to wiggle, One tummy to jiggle,
One eye to wink, Two eyes to blink,
One foot to hop, Two feet to jump,
Five fingers to wriggle, Ten fingers to tickle,
Now see what YOU can do!

Beverley Michael.

Here comes daddy

First comes daddy with his great big feet,
Marching, marching down the street.
Swinging his arms, with his head held high,
Never stopping as he passes by.

Now comes mummy with her dancing feet,
Twirling, twirling, down the street.
She waves her arms while on her tiptoes,
Jigging like this wherever she goes.

Look, here's the son with his football feet,
Kicking, kicking, down the street.
The fastest feet you have ever seen,
Scoring goals for his favourite team.

Next comes the daughter with her skipping feet,
Bobbing, bobbing, down the street.
Her knees bounce high as she swings along,
Singing her very own skipping song.

Here comes grandma with her tired old feet,
Shuffling, shuffling, down the street.
With her back so bent, she walks with a stick,
Always slowly, tip, tap, tip.

Last comes the baby with his tiny little feet,
Crawling, crawling, down the street.
He tries to toddle, but he always falls,
Because a baby can't walk well at all.

Beverley Michael.

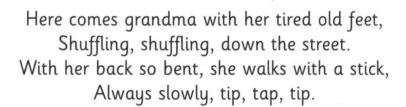

I can ...

Tick the boxes when you can do these actions.

I can <u>c</u>atch a ball

I can <u>s</u>kip

I can <u>b</u>alance on one foot

I can <u>h</u>op

I can gallop

I can <u>r</u>oll

Twinkling stars

Draw a line between two stars with the same number of points.

Sing the rhyme

Sing the nursery rhymes in the pictures while moving a part of your body to the beat.